This book was a catalyst for our board
vision while empowering the school's s
a clear understanding of roles and resp
to this recommended resource.

Derek Maat, Board Chair, and George Petrusma, Principal,
John Knox Christian School, Ontario, Canada

Len Stob provides a philosophical overview along with detailed instruction on how to
implement change. We know from personal experience that mission-directed governance
can transform your board meetings and strengthen your head-of-school / board relationship,
resulting in shared vision and dynamic progress.

Wendy Hofman, Head of School, and Gillian Granger, President of the Board of Trustees,
Lansing Christian School, Lansing, Michigan

Over the past several years the board of directors for Ontario Christian School has been
utilizing Mr. Stob's book to help guide and direct its specific role and its corresponding
responsibilities and duties. Purposely implementing the mission-directed model has been
vital in developing a board culture of greater unity and purpose, which then accelerates board
leadership effectiveness.

Brad Verhoeven, President of the Board of Trustees,
Ontario Christian Schools, Ontario, California

How can Christian schools operate in ways that meaningfully connect mission and best
practice? Stob's keen insight and wisdom, gained from years of experience, will prove to be
very valuable for Christian education leaders. His clear priority is implementing structures
and policies that keep first things first by promoting sound teaching, learning, and student
discipleship. I heartily recommend this highly perceptive and helpful book to all Christian
school administrators and boards!

Dan Beerens, Educational Consultant and Senior Fellow,
Center for the Advancement of Christian Education

In *Mission Directed*, Leonard Stob demonstrates the craft of Christian school governance
leadership—not only in his message but also by example. Throughout the book, he engages his
readers to reflect deeply about the wisdom of Christian school governance structures, and he
does so by modeling his own refinement of reflection in an improved second edition. His vison
for mission-directed governance is a clarion call for Christian schools looking for changes to
their governance model as they recognize the need for their institutions to flourish.

Julius de Jager, Executive Director, Ontario Alliance of Christian Schools,
Hamilton, Ontario, Canada.

To Sharon.

Thank you for being a true partner in this ministry for God's glory.

MISSION
Directed

Governing your Christian school
with purpose

Leonard Stob

© 2015 by Leonard Stob

Purposeful Design Publications is the publishing division of the Association of Christian Schools International (ACSI) and is committed to the ministry of Christian school education, to enable Christian educators and schools worldwide to effectively prepare students for life. As the publisher of textbooks, trade books, and other educational resources within ACSI, Purposeful Design Publications strives to produce biblically sound materials that reflect Christian scholarship and stewardship and that address the identified needs of Christian schools around the world.

The views expressed in this publication are those of the author, and they may not necessarily represent the position of the Association of Christian Schools International.

Unless otherwise identified, all Scripture quotations are taken from the Holy Bible, NEW INTERNATIONAL VERSION®. Copyright © 1973, 1978, 1984, 2011 by Biblica, Inc. All rights reserved worldwide. Used by permission of Biblica, Inc.

Printed in the United States of America
20 19 18 17 16 15   1 2 3 4 5 6 7

Stob, Leonard
Mission directed: Governing your Christian school with purpose
Second edition
ISBN 978-1-58331-551-4   Catalog #9597
Design team: David Bates, Mike Riester
Editorial team: John Conaway, Frieda Nossaman
Cover Image: Thinkstock.com

Originally published as *Mission-Directed Governance,* Calvin College Press, 2011.

Purposeful Design Publications
A Division of ACSI
PO Box 65130 • Colorado Springs, CO 80962-5130

Customer Service: 800-367-0798 • www.acsi.org

CONTENTS

FOREWORD

A key question facing Christian school leaders and communities today is, Will Christian schooling be relevant for the next generation? Cultural, demographic, and technological changes have resulted in a "new normal" environment that Christian school leaders must navigate to ensure the sustainability of their schools. Economic realities, diminishing church support, and the increasingly consumeristic mentality of Christian parents have changed the decision-making and leadership landscape for heads of schools and boards. If Christian schools are to flourish today and be there for our "children's children," they must look beyond the status quo to more effective models, structures, and philosophies that will enable them to keep pace with a rapidly changing world. As organizational management guru Gary Hamel said, "Organizations lose their relevance when the rate of internal change lags the pace of external change."

Many Christian schools operate under a governance model that has been in place since the inception of their school—with little change or innovation. Board committees, board meeting agendas, and roles and expectations remain essentially the same. They tend to be "problem-solving boards" that focus on "what is" rather than "what can be." Decision making tends to be either reactive (solving a problem) or random (keeping up with the school down the street). We live, lead, and govern in times that demand a change from the status quo to more effective governance models and performance. Significant change has also impacted the role of the head of school and the head's relationship with the school board.

An effective and flourishing Christian school board must fulfill three primary objectives: uphold and support the mission and vision of the school, advance the strategic future of the school, and provide for the financial security and sustainability of the school. It must be able to clearly and demonstrably determine what must not change, what should change, and how change will be implemented. It must work diligently to establish and maintain a relationship with the head of school founded on the essentials: vision, mission, core values, and strategic plans and initiatives.

Leonard Stob presents a governance model that effectively builds on the Christian foundation, philosophy, and heritage of Christian schools while reshaping the work of the board "for such a time as this." All Christian school boards would be well served—perhaps transformed—by effectively answering the three critical questions for evaluating a school's governance model: (1) How does the school identify and protect its foundational beliefs? (2) How does the school develop and promote its vision and mission? (3) How does the school identify the roles of those in authority, determine the process for decision making, and ensure accountability?

I have found that using these questions to direct decision making, leadership relationships, and policy development moves the board away from problem solving and task orientation to strategic thinking and action. Strategic plans, annual goals, and head-of-school and board evaluations are established on a strong foundation that provides clear direction, unity of purpose, and a means to determine what defines success. The mission-driven model removes ambiguity in the relationship between the board and head of school regarding the most essential leadership roles and responsibilities. Enhanced clarity and unity strengthen the leadership relationships and lead to longer-tenured and more-successful heads of school.

I would encourage Christian school boards to use *Mission Driven* as a board training and assessment tool. Stob has used his experience as the head of a Christian school that developed and implemented the mission-driven model to provide helpful illustrations, keen insights, and thought-provoking questions that will catalyze reflection, discussion, and goal setting. Boards that practice continuous learning might use a portion of board meetings throughout the year to discuss Stob's mission-driven model.

I commend Leonard Stob for taking a leading role in presenting a new model for Christian school governance that is well suited for these "new normal" times for Christian schooling. I have shared Stob's book with many Christian school leaders since the first edition was published in 2011, and look forward to using this revised edition while serving the cause of Christian schooling in the years ahead.

James C. Marsh, Jr., Director of the Van Lunen Center
Calvin College/Grand Rapids, Michigan
Head of School Emeritus, Westminster Christian Academy
St. Louis, Missouri

PREFACE

My motivation for writing this book is to serve the kingdom of Christ by presenting a governance model to help Christian schools more consistently, purposefully, and successfully advance Christian education.

I have served as teacher and school head in Christian schools that were under various forms of the traditional governance model. I was privileged to serve with many profoundly dedicated board members, administrators, faculty, and staff who loved the Lord and wanted the best for the school. Hundreds of students were trained in Christian practices, relationships, and worldview. These students now serve the Lord throughout the world in their myriad vocations; they also bring Christ's rule to bear in their families, churches, and communities.

As an active school head, I thought a lot about governance models. I was most familiar with what I call the traditional governance model; however my experiences and observations indicated some shortcomings with this model—issues that in some cases had the potential of causing harm to the school. In the late 1990s I began to explore the governance-by-policy model; however, though it was an improvement over the traditional model in some respects, I saw potential problems with that model as well. Those experiences led me to develop a governance model which I believe combines the strengths of both models while avoiding, or at least mitigating, potential weaknesses. I call this model the mission-directed governance model.

The first school to officially adopt the mission-directed governance model was Ontario Christian School in Ontario, California, where I was head of school. The board approved the development of a mission-directed governance model, and after a year it officially adopted the model. At the same time, we redesigned the curriculum to more purposefully and deliberately train children and young adults in Christian discipleship.

It is important to acknowledge the board, administrative team, and faculty of Ontario Christian School. I give special thanks to Mark Lambooy and Bernie Vander Molen for their leadership on the board in those early years. Those who have studied the process of change know that major modifications can come only with the active support of those who are enlisted to carry out the mandates. The first line of change was to come with the Ontario Christian administrative team. They translated to the faculty what was happening and why, and secured the involvement that brought about the changes. The faculty and staff responded in outstanding ways to make many creative and meaningful contributions to Christian education. Thank you, John Voortman, for your support and active leadership in bolstering visionary ideas when there were doubts and when progress seemed to stall.

I give special thanks to Carolyn Cooper, curriculum director. She has made an outstanding impact in leading faculty through complicated discussions on how to more effectively make the curriculum a focused and purposeful extension of the mission. As my daughter, she has also volunteered countless personal hours to review several editions of the manuscript of this book. She has provided many observations about how to apply the mission-directed governance model, especially to the curriculum and to student learning. She offered excellent advice to improve this second edition.

The administrative team first suggested I write this book. We knew the day would come for me to retire from serving as the head of school. This book could provide board members, administrators, and faculty with a continuing rationale, description, and explanation of the mission-directed governance model that the school had adopted and that all had worked so hard to bring about.

Modifications and improvements were made in both the curriculum and the mission-directed governance model over the next few years. As I retired from my service to this school, the board and administrators have unanimously confirmed their commitment to continue both the mission and the mission-directed governance model.

There are many people who had major roles in contributing to this book. There are those who gave their experience and good judgment on the concepts. Many experienced Christian school head administrators, as well as college professors who have served as Christian school administrators and are involved in research in Christian education, offered their feedback. The list includes those who have witnessed a broad variety of Christian schools during their service as Christian school board members, leaders of accreditation teams, educational consultants, and in other critical roles.

Let me name and say thank you to a few individuals, experienced Christian school administrators who have read and evaluated earlier editions of the book and given their insights: Ryan Zonnefeld, Dan Beerens, Jim Marsh, Don Holwerda, Larry Kooi, and Jack Postma. Their observations led to major changes in the manuscript in order to elaborate certain points, reduce duplication, and sharpen the focus. These colleagues helped ensure that the ideas made sense and accurately resonated with the experiences of those in the education business.

Thanks for those involved in this second edition. I especially appreciate the influence and advice of Dr. Derek Keenan, of the Association of Christian Schools International, Steven Babbitt, of Purposeful Design Publications, and the weeks of editing work by John Conaway.

There are those with whom I have had discussions who were encouraging when it seemed the project would never be completed. Often they would introduce me to others who had a fresh perspective. Thanks to Paul Luchtenburg, John Kieft, Chris Johnson, and Virginia Vander Hart. I must give a note of special appreciation to the encouragement for doing Christian education on purpose that I received from discussions and visits with John Perkins.

Let me express lasting appreciation to Dr. Shirley Roels, who strongly encouraged and promoted the first edition of this work. Thank you to Dr. David I. Smith, director of the Kuyers Institute for Christian Teaching and Learning at Calvin College, who edited the first edition of the manuscript.

And finally, I must express humble thanks to my wonderful wife, Sharon, and my family. Sharon gave countless words of encouragement to help me see the project through to the end in spite of her having to endure many hours of loud music as I worked in the study most evenings and weekends. My children and their spouses were fabulous cheerleaders and encouragers. Thanks to Jeff and Stephanie Cooper, Nathan and Tessa Stob, Jamieson and Alison Wierenga, and Josh and Carolyn Cooper.

I pray that this project will glorify God and help Christian schools promote the growth of whole-life Christian disciples.

INTRODUCTION

You probably are reading this book because you have a leadership role in a Christian school. You may be a board member or school head, or have another leadership role. You most likely are a person of integrity, have a strong work ethic and a willingness to serve, are committed to the foundational beliefs of the school, are dedicated to seeing the ministry prosper, and have high ideals.

You may be generally pleased with the performance of the school board and administrative leaders, and you may be enthusiastic about the current and future direction of the school. But many school leaders face serious concerns. Are the school board and the head of school leading the school toward a focused goal, or are they simply managing day-to-day crises in an attempt to slow what looks like an inevitable decline? Is the school open to innovation and vision, or does it assume a business-as-usual mind-set? Does the board have general unity regarding the school's mission, or are board meetings marked by power struggles and a clash of personal agendas?

Even if you have positive feelings about the school, you may be concerned about various issues. How effectively does the school guide students toward lives of discipleship? How well does the curriculum integrate biblical truth with academic subjects? How well has the school prepared to face the challenge of societal change? What can school leadership do to enhance the school's relevance and viability for the long term? How can the school stay true to its core beliefs and principles and still address changing student needs? How can the school attract leaders and teachers of excellence? How can the school leadership communicate the school's mission and vision to community members and organizations?

When a Christian school is stuck on a plateau, it is most often due to the school's organizational structure and how that structure enables or restricts leaders' ability to handle vision, mission, authority, accountability, and the process of decision making. These are the key topics of governance. The school's governance model needs to release leaders from the distractions of day-to-day issues so that they can concentrate on the mission they are pledged to advance. The governance model needs to provide a way to hold the school leaders accountable for carrying out this mission.

This book introduces, describes, and advocates for the *mission-directed governance model*. This model is designed to help a school identify and advance its mission and provide focused accountability while holding fast to its essential positions of faith and philosophy. The purpose is to help leaders of Christian schools more effectively address organization, purpose, and priority through an organizational structure that will challenge familiar traditions and culture. Under the mission-directed governance model the school will be encouraged to define its ideals and to more consciously focus and coordinate every aspect of the organization toward accomplishing its mission and vision. Following this model can liberate and motivate leaders, faculty, and staff and reduce internal conflicts and politics. It also provides a basis for obtaining measurable results. This model focuses all dimensions of the Christian school on accomplishing the school's stated purpose.

Developing and implementing the mission-directed governance model is intended to be an ongoing process that is always improving. This book is not meant to end discussion on governance, nor is the mission-directed model a rigid archetype that schools must follow in every detail. While not the definitive answer, the mission-directed governance model does take discussion and thinking about governance to a new level, with high expectations for Christian school leaders to offer purposeful Christian education that will get chosen results. A school's governance model will determine how the school identifies and resolves school issues. A sound governance model is especially critical in a rapidly changing societal and cultural landscape that continually tests a school's assumptions and requires fresh responses.

Experience shows that the mission-directed governance model can help a school maintain stability of its core philosophical positions while also encouraging the school to seek creative measures that advance the school's mission—enabling agile and flexible decision making within defined limits.

THE PLAN OF THE BOOK

Every Christian school needs a mission and a process by which to organize its decision making and planning. This book makes the case that the mission-directed governance model is able to help schools accomplish this objective more effectively than other governance models.

Part 1 of the book asserts that a school's governance model is a major factor in the way the school operates in and responds to a rapidly changing school environment. There are changes in the community, culture, political situation, and economy that the school cannot control but that can significantly affect school operations and priorities; the school's governance model determines how the school handles such changes.

The following three school governance models are compared and contrasted: the traditional governance model, the governance-by-policy model, and the mission-directed governance model. The following three critical questions are addressed for each model to help the reader evaluate each model and its implications:

1. How does the school identify and protect its foundational beliefs?

2. How does the school develop and promote its vision and mission?

3. How does the school identify the roles of those in authority, determine the process for decision making, and ensure accountability?

Part 2 fleshes out the mission-directed model of governance. This governance model is designed to be effective for any Christian school—parochial (or church-owned), independently owned by an association of parents, or owned by an individual or small group. It is appropriate for schools of any grade level. Whether the school's mission is evangelism, discipleship, classical education, or college preparatory training, this governance model can help the board and head of school guide the school effectively.

Part 3 concentrates on specific strategies for advancing the school's mission, beginning with board governance of student learning. The vision for the Christian school is to purposefully cultivate a comprehensive learning community in which all aspects of the school are tied together for the advancement of the mission. Other strategies include governing school culture, measuring critical aspects of the school, building a mission-focused budget, and establishing an appropriate relationship between the board and the head of school.

Part 4 reviews key elements of the mission-directed governance model and provides helpful suggestions for a school that wants to transition to this governance model.

At the end of each chapter are questions for reflection and discussion. While this book can be beneficial for an individual reader, it is purposefully structured for use as a training manual for school board members. These questions can be useful for stimulating group discussion and bringing helpful consensus.

The school's governance model must do more than provide a way for the board to work cooperatively and make wise decisions about current problems. It should also provide the structure and the means by which the school can purposefully accomplish its mission with vision, unity, and accountability. The goal of this book is to help Christian school leaders nurture students to be committed to Jesus Christ as Savior and Lord and prepared for works of service that advance His kingdom. The thesis of this book is that the mission-directed governance model provides the most effective way to ensure that a Christian school achieves its mission.

PART ONE

The Primary Issue:
Governance

CHAPTER 1

How Change Is Challenging Your School

School leaders desire their schools to be living examples of excellence. They dream of a board and administration that work as a team striving to make a common vision a reality. What would the results be if leaders continuously and harmoniously strove to make this ministry a model of its ideals? What would it be like if there were a clear vision and understanding of what students are to learn? What if the board spent minimal time on routine problems and instead prioritized thinking about the future with a long-range plan and strategy? This can be more than a dream; it is possible.

Today's Christian schools are buffeted by continuous waves of change. Many changes are out of the control of school leaders—for example, demographic changes in the community such as economic growth or decline. New people moving into the community and joining the school create opportunity but also are an unknown factor. These people new to the school are enthusiastic about Christian education and want to participate; however, they may find that they are not always welcomed in decision-making roles because they don't know the school's history, the standing and influence of the families in the school community, or why the school follows its current practices.

Even in relatively stable communities, changes in technology expose families to new ideas, worldwide issues in economics and education, and shifting attitudes regarding what should be tolerated, protected, or promoted. In many communities there are changes in attitudes toward religion in general and Christianity in particular.

Another source of strain may be increased competition from other schooling models such as home education, charter schools, public schools, specialized public schools, and online education. Families may think that Christian schooling is not worth the cost if the primary distinction is Bible stories, devotions, and chapel. And the tuition for Christian schools will never be as low as public or charter schools or home education.

School morale and expectations are also subject to change. The founders of a Christian school likely had a vision of the school as a ministry. Whether the school was established by a church, a committed group of parents, or some other body, there were high hopes for success. However, over time the spirit of sacrifice can subside. Perhaps the school has settled into a familiar pattern reflecting the expectations of a homogeneous community. Or perhaps the school has experienced stress when original aspirations (such as enrollment projections or keeping costs low) did not materialize. Perhaps a church, parents, or certain donors were expected to subsidize the effort, but that source of support has diminished. For a number of reasons, the euphoria of early enthusiasm may have subsided, and thus the school community no longer has the same sense of confidence.

As a result of such changes, school leaders can no longer take for granted the practices of a predictable, homogeneous community. Schools have always struggled with changes in technology, teaching methods, media, and the ever-present financial burden, but the impact of these issues appears to be increasing. Even schools that have enjoyed long-term support are challenged in new ways.

Some Christian schools are concentrating only on survival. There certainly are many Christian schools facing severe conditions, if not outright crises. Scores of Christian schools close their doors each year. In addition, dozens of administrators and principals are fired or leave the profession.

Because of these changes and trends, school leaders find that what had been assumed is now being challenged. Even with highly motivated and competent leaders, it is hard to find consensus as to what course to take. Issues can become political, with constituents forming polarized groups that lobby board members, administrators, and the broader school community. With increased anxiety comes more arguing in board meetings; motions might pass not because there is consensus but because someone finally gives up his or her position out of frustration. The one thing board members can agree on is that the board is dealing with too many day-to-day issues rather than concentrating on larger concerns. They admit that the board is reacting to issues rather than promoting a united plan for advancement.

Amid deepening challenges, leaders wonder whether there are ways to improve the school's slow response to changing conditions and its tendency to maintain the status quo. Is it possible to find ways to identify and solve problems? Can one dare to hope to prevent problems? Or is there something about Christian schools that ties them to mediocrity? Do these challenges call only for more prayer for God's intervention in the external environment, or do they also call for school leaders to prayerfully consider doing something different?

THE SCHOOL NEEDS TO ADDRESS CHANGE

A major challenge for a Christian school is to figure out how the school will manage change and bring an orderly, purposeful direction to the ministry. Differences in approach are evident when the school approaches hard issues, particularly when there are financial or philosophical implications.

Faced with such changes, a school board member might say, "It's time we ran this ministry like a business!" This statement typically is uttered in an exasperated tone late at night after intense discussion of issues such as what to do about deficit spending or about families that are behind in paying tuition. It is a plea for efficiency and an appeal to make decisions for the good of the school.

This suggestion often comes from those who insist that the school must be more responsive to present and potential customers. Those who hold this position may offer arguments like the following. First, a business approach will produce greater quality and consistency, resulting in higher academic scores, improvements in facilities and services, a better financial outlook, better-motivated and better-paid employees, real accountability, and an opportunity to get out of the mire of mediocrity. Second, the school must be relevant to the community and the external environment, and so must adopt a consumer-market mentality. The school must adjust to meet the shifting wants and needs of consumers, or else it will no longer have enough students to make the endeavor worthwhile. In commercial terms, the "niche" is shrinking; anticipating the desires of potential customers and implementing creative innovations might entice new families to join the school and help the school avoid irrelevance.

On the other hand, some Christian school leaders feel that running the ministry "like a business" is akin to uttering a vulgarity. Isn't a business style an apparent abandonment of ministry in concession to worldly criteria? "Customer," "product," or "market" may connote an irreverent, impersonal, uncaring approach and should not be used in the same sentence as Christian ministry. Such a proposal, they feel, is in flagrant contradiction to trusting God and putting faith in God's care. It risks putting love and compassion on hold and trampling on people's deeper needs and feelings. Attempting to apply business practices seems to imply a path of cold calculation to enhance the bottom line. This seems contrary to the commitment that the Christian school ministry must come under the authority of Jesus Christ. These school leaders are open to some changes but insist that the Christian ministry must preserve its essential beliefs and characteristics. Their concern is that if the school changes it might compromise the essence of its ministry. Those who resist change see their role as the preservers of truth and of the essential philosophical principles of the school. They caution against consumerism with its mentality of allowing change for change's sake, and so their resistance to change is not just ducking responsible action. They perceive the need to move confidently in a productive direction, rather than just flailing to show activity.

The problem, then, is not the motivation of those who hold either position. Those on both sides want strong, vigorous Christian schools. The one side wants to ensure the Christian school will continue to serve and be relevant. The other side emphasizes the need to preserve the essential characteristics of the gospel and Christian education.

To resolve this dilemma, the leaders of the Christian school must recognize the truth in both arguments. This is a both/and situation, not either/or. The school must protect and preserve its founding principles and advance the Christian ministry. The leaders not only must identify how to be responsive to the Holy Spirit's leading, but they also must plan strategically, strive for goals, and develop systematic ways of measuring and achieving those goals. Changes that respond to consumer demands must not compromise the founding beliefs and purpose. The Christian school needs to anticipate and plan for change. In addition, the school must be a faithful steward of its resources while providing a high-quality education that reflects positively on the name of Christ and is attractive to families.

The school must be accountable both for achieving its purposes and goals, and also for its assets, resources, and people. Before the school can achieve meaningful goals that advance the school's larger educational aims, it is necessary to first draw a clear consensus on what is the nature and purpose of Christian schooling. As the school gains a clear direction, it makes sense to evaluate available governance models to determine which model most effectively allows the school leadership to achieve the mission. The school needs to educate on purpose.

THE CENTRAL ISSUE IS GOVERNANCE

It is apparent that how the school handles change will affect its organizational life, its decision-making process, and the nature and amount of conflict it experiences. How the school handles change is critical. The school must be able to identify what must not change and what can change, and it must establish an appropriate process for making changes.

The governance model under which the school operates is critical to the health and direction of the school. The school's governance model is the framework that determines the process of decision making and, therefore, how the institution will handle change.

The governance structure provides the reins for control and determines who is empowered to set direction and decide on operational practices. The model clarifies the roles of the board, the head of school, and the owner. It also clarifies the degree of their participation and influence, the limits of their authority and decision making, and the degree of their accountability. The governance model determines which issues the school will consider as well as the process by which the school can anticipate, evaluate, discuss, and resolve those issues. Most importantly, the governance model determines whether those who hold leadership positions can provide real leadership.

Before comparing governance models and analyzing how well each model introduces meaningful change and prevents distracting change, it is necessary to determine the purpose of the education the school is establishing. Then it will be more appropriate to consider governance models and how they help school leaders address change. Each governance model produces distinctive expectations as to what issues are appropriate to discuss and what the process for change should be.

FOR REFLECTION AND DISCUSSION

1. What are some of the changes your school is facing right now? Think of changes in the community, the constituency of the school, the local

economic situation, the school's relationship with local churches, and any other relevant changes. Also discuss broader issues: societal change, the national economy, the school's history and heritage, the ability of the school to anticipate and respond to change, and so on.

2. As you've observed the way the school has been led and managed, what are the school's organizational strengths? How do you think the school could become more efficient and effective? What corporate practices do you think the school should consider in order for it to work more efficiently? What aspects of the school operation (for instance, human resources, planning, marketing, facilities) could benefit from business expertise?

3. In your opinion, has the school modified its mission since its founding? Describe some of those changes, and discuss the reasons for those changes. If the school has not shifted its original mission, discuss why it has maintained its key features. Also discuss whether some of those founding features are up for discussion.

CHAPTER 2

What to Look for in a Governance Model

In order for a Christian school to run well, leaders must not assume that people and resources will automatically come together or work well on their own. Any success is the result of conscious hard work, with a community of people understanding the cause and moving in the same direction.

Even with clear assignments and timelines, goals can fade and organizational plans can unravel as participants shift their attention to other concerns, priorities, and distractions. Without strong, visionary leadership, the situation can slide toward disorder. If the leadership is not headed toward an identifiable target, there can be organizational drift from founding principles; there can be impulsive decisions based on expediency or on wrong criteria. Christian schools need leaders who understand a biblical perspective on the purpose of education, leaders who are principled and exhibit servant-leadership, and an organizational structure that brings vision, unity, and accountability.

Each governance model brings a different view of the board's role and how it should make decisions. These views influence the style, culture, and expectation of what are appropriate relationships and how the school should operate. What should those looking for quality Christian education hope for in school leadership? Christians immediately think of Jesus' teaching on leadership to His disciples in passages such as these:

> Sitting down, Jesus called the Twelve and said, "Anyone who wants to be first must be the very last, and the servant of all." (Mark 9:35)

> Jesus called them together and said, "You know that those who are regarded as rulers of the Gentiles lord it over them, and their high officials exercise authority over them. Not so with you. Instead, whoever wants to become great among you must be your servant, and whoever wants to be first must be slave of all. For even the Son of Man did not come to be served, but to serve, and to give his life as a ransom for many." (Mark 10:42–45)

The apostle Paul instructs Timothy as follows:

> Don't have anything to do with foolish and stupid arguments, because you know they produce quarrels. And the Lord's servant must not be quarrelsome but must be kind to everyone, able to teach, not resentful. (2 Timothy 2:23–24)

Certainly these teachings apply to the personal motivations of those who would serve in positions of leadership. It is necessary for leaders of Christian organizations to be living examples of what Christ calls for in those who have authority to give guidance and direction. It would be counter to such basic principles to have school leaders who are striving for personal power and influence or those who bring adversarial attitudes. The selection process should put in place board members who are trustees of the whole ministry, not people who are argumentative or who come with an agenda or who focus on a specific issue. Governance should bring leaders to the school who are trustees; therefore, in this book references to *board members* will be interchangeable with *trustees* and *school board* with *board* and *board of trustees*.

But beyond personal motivation, all those associated with the school want the organization to be a place where servant-leaders have a structure, process, and culture that support their commitment to make decisions that are best for all aspects of the ministry. It is important for the school to have board members who are living examples of servant-leadership.

The board must bring vision. The school has a purpose that is bigger than any leader. The school leaders must be people who acknowledge and serve Jesus as Savior and Lord. School leaders must see the ministry as an opportunity to serve and glorify God. They oversee what is being done in order to establish and ensure appropriate practices. Such practices are necessary if the school is to obey the will of God, glorify God, and advance His kingdom.

The board must bring unity. The school is a community trying to achieve a common purpose as described in the vision and mission statements. School leaders, parents, and employees must be motivated to accomplish the mission and understand their role, and they must be willing to sacrifice to further the cause.

The board must bring accountability. All Christians confess that they are sinners and are accountable to God. But everyone, even the school board, should be accountable to other people as well. Accountability brings four things. (1) Accountability can prevent problems because the leaders of the organization are measuring specific aspects of the school and have policies in place for regular inspection of school's processes. (2) Accountability can protect the individuals making decisions by identifying and solving problems while they are small, thus sparing the individuals from gossip and avoiding the need for public correction. (3) Accountability that corrects problems can result in improvement. (4) Accountability does not have merely a negative function (e.g., identifying what is wrong); it also provides opportunities for praise, celebration, and affirmation.

The school's governance model should encourage the school's leaders to concentrate on moving confidently toward advancing the mission, with methods in place to resolve routine problems. The governance model should provide the board with a way to apply proactive strategies rather than just reacting to the most recently identified problems.

The most critical problems—the ones that cause the most damage—are usually associated with the school's organization and its expectations, limitations, and processes. School problems are not primarily people problems. There may be an occasional cantankerous or inept person, but the crucial problems typically are not the result of the motivations, work ethic, intelligence, or loyalty of board members, administrators, staff, or constituents. Everyone involved wants what is best for the school and hopes to contribute to its success. Boards are tempted to think that the answer to problems is to get a new school head, a new board member, or a new teacher—if only to send the message that they are seriously addressing the issues. Firing good people will not help develop a good school. The right people with the right training and experience need to be in the right positions and be willing to participate with a clear mandate, an understood process, and explicit accountability.

The school's governance model should include the following characteristics:

- Articulates a clear philosophy and mission
- Focuses the school's attention and energies on advancing the mission
- Identifies, protects, and promotes the organization's core values

- Provides an orderly decision-making process

- Designates roles of authority

- Articulates a clear, unified, and consistent understanding of purpose, expectations, and operations (policies)

- Ensures that the board and administration have accurate, necessary, meaningful, and full information for decision making

- Provides an organizational structure that promotes stewardship, efficiency, financial stability, and strategic planning

- Includes a process for all participants to contribute to the mission within their defined roles

- Provides measurable objectives and the means to measure progress

- Ensures accountability of all participants, with identified responsibilities and limits of authority

- Enjoys confident and supportive relationships, produced by unity in direction and priority

THREE CRITICAL QUESTIONS

The goal of this book is to propose a governance model that enables the board to articulate a mission that has integrity with its founding beliefs, but also guides the board to provide effective policies and processes. This governance model aims to help school leaders make informed decisions and plans that purposefully advance and align the school's curriculum, programs, operations, and relationships toward accomplishing the school's stated mission. It is designed to bring vision, unity, and accountability.

It is important to have clear criteria by which to evaluate governance models. This book will compare and contrast three school governance models. Each model will be analyzed according to the same criteria. These criteria are embodied in three critical questions, which will be addressed for each governance model.

QUESTION 1: How does the school identify and protect its foundational beliefs?

Each school needs to define the foundational beliefs and purposes upon which it stands and ensure that they remain secure and relevant. This book considers the effectiveness of each model in identifying the school's foundational principles and beliefs and providing walls of protection against changing them.

When considering the pressures of change, the school needs to articulate the faith and purpose positions to which it is anchored and on which it will not compromise. These will be referred to as the school's nonnegotiables. A clear, written identification of the nonnegotiables and a model that provides for their protection will allow schools to more freely consider change in other areas, assured that the most critical areas are safe from modification.

QUESTION 2: How does the school identify and promote its mission and vision?

The school also needs to determine the ideal it is striving to reach. Identifying the ideal offers a basis for evaluating present curriculum, educational experiences, and school operations; it also provides school leaders with the motivation and direction for proactively initiating change. The school's leaders need a common understanding of philosophy, mission, and vision.

A healthy school will have a consistent theology, philosophy, and mission that bring unity in purpose and goals. A dynamic school governance model ensures that the vision and mission give direction to all aspects of the school. The answer to this question enables us to evaluate how effectively each model focuses on the school's mission and cultivates its vision in a manner consistent with its philosophy.

QUESTION 3: How does the school identify the roles of authority, determine the process for decision making, and ensure accountability?

Each school has ways of determining which issues it will consider, who has the authority to make which decisions, and the process by which decisions will be made. To evaluate each governance model, we will consider the effectiveness of the process that schools following that model would use to determine roles, incorporate accountability, set priorities, resolve issues, and manage change—while protecting the nonnegotiables and promoting the mission.

A robust school governance model designates decision-making roles and responsibilities and ensures accountability. School operational processes work within and as an extension of the governance framework to accomplish the school's goals.

There are a number of school governance models. Many models reflect particular local and historical circumstances. However, most school governance models fit loosely into one of two patterns: the traditional governance model and the governance-by-policy model.

To effectively evaluate school governance models, it will be important to consider how they address each of the three critical issues presented in the questions above: preserving nonnegotiables, advancing the vision and mission, and providing a meaningful and efficient process of decision making. After describing and evaluating the traditional model and the governance-by-policy model, a third model—the mission-directed governance model—will be introduced.

FOR REFLECTION AND DISCUSSION

1. Why is governance critical to a school?

2. Why is it important for a school to be intentional about its governance model? How does the choice of governance model affect a school?

3. How does your school identify and protect its foundational beliefs?

4. How does your school identify and promote its mission and vision?

5. What decision-making processes and procedures are followed by your school leaders? What have been some positive and negative effects of those practices?

CHAPTER 3

Characteristics of the Traditional Governance Model

The traditional model of governance is common in Christian schools. Historically, the traditional governance model has been a community affair, with the school board handling daily school concerns as representatives of a homogeneous community.

Today a Christian school most likely operates under an owner such as a church, a small group of investors, or an association composed of parents and friends of the school. Each school's governance structure has unique features, of course, but there are some common characteristics of schools that operate under the traditional governance model. Each of these characteristics has both strengths and weaknesses.

1. PURPOSES OF THE BOARD

The school board is composed of individuals who make decisions on behalf of the school. Board members are committed to the purposes of the school and sincerely work for its success. However, the board's function under the traditional governance model has some inherent weaknesses. Sometimes members serve as representatives of churches or other supporting organizations, which could result in divided loyalty. The board's purpose is to consider school issues and make decisions based on consensus and compromise; the danger is that board members may lack the courage to make tough decisions or may defer authority to other parties. There are usually some written school positions such as a statement of faith, a faculty handbook, or a student handbook; however, there may be few written policies that guide the board itself or the decision-making process. The traditional governance model is usually characterized by having many standing committees, which may result in unclear chains of authority.

2. STANDING COMMITTEES

To build consensus, the school often invites school community members to serve on board-established standing committees. The standing committees are intended to build community, loyalty, and support by having decisions made by members of the broader school constituency. Typical examples include standing committees for education, facilities, transportation, technology, finance, promotion, development or fund raising, and long-range planning. These committees are often composed of one or two school board members, a few parents, and perhaps a teacher or two. The head of school and other administrators are expected to be present, but often in a nonvoting, advisory capacity.

The job of the committees and the board includes listening to the constituency to identify problems, and then to recommend to the board a plan to fix the problem. The traditional model ensures that committees and the board are involved in most decisions, even those involving daily operations of the school. Committee and board members may even be directly involved in interviewing and hiring teachers, making observations in the classroom, and evaluating current teachers. They may be involved in interviewing new families and in determining penalties in student discipline cases. A standing committee usually determines its own agenda for the year by determining the problems and areas of concern that the committee members are interested in solving. After much discussion, the committee forms a recommendation that it forwards to the board.

Experience shows that this approach can have undesirable consequences.

- A standing committee can challenge the role and authority of the school board. It is not uncommon for a standing committee to become more politically powerful than the board. If a committee submits a recommendation to the board, the political expectation is that the board will approve the recommendation. Although board members may ask a few questions for clarification, the board usually is not in a position to challenge the recommendation because the committee has more thoroughly studied the issue and has received firsthand reports. Since committees often include teachers and other constituency representatives, their recommendations and rationale may be known to the public before they are presented to the board. If the board rejects a committee's recommendation, the public rift may cause the constituency to choose sides. This puts pressure on the board to rubber-stamp the recommendation or be prepared for potentially embarrassing public confrontation.

- A standing committee rarely considers long-term strategic issues. A standing committee typically determines its agenda by identifying perceived problems rather than by focusing on advancing the mission of the school. Moreover, since a standing committee may change members or chairpersons each year, it rarely considers issues that will require more than one year to resolve. If the board's agenda depends on reports and recommendations from reactive standing committees, the board is unlikely to face long-term strategic issues either.

- The owner or board doesn't necessarily select members of standing committees; committee members are usually chosen by the committee chairperson, historical precedent, or other process outside of board approval. There may be controversy over who serves on a committee and the roles they play. There likely are no formal rules to define terms of office, so there is no official process for removing an unproductive or overbearing member from a standing committee.

- Standing committees are sometimes organized in ways that challenge the role and authority of the school head. Since teachers often serve on these committees, and the committees may be prone to support the teachers and their ideas for improvement, teachers serving on committees may introduce issues without consulting the school head—or perhaps even with the knowledge that the administrator does not support the proposal. This places the school head in a dilemma— ignore the challenge, or publicly disagree with the teacher. By opposing the proposal, the head of school may appear uninformed and unsupportive of faculty desires. This can create an awkward political situation in which the teacher in practice becomes the spokesperson for the faculty, especially as the teacher is often a voting committee member and the administrator an advisor. The teacher becomes the teacher "representative" for the whole faculty at committee meetings; in time, other teachers will likely bring their concerns directly to this teacher, bypassing the administrator and confusing lines of authority, communication, and accountability. This changes the power structure and risks developing a culture of distrust between faculty and administrators. This also means that teachers who are directly affected by an issue do not offer observations; instead, they must depend on the teacher representative to speak on their behalf.

- Standing committees often produce inaction and ineffectual compromise. The culture of standing committees is designed to maintain the status quo and prevent radical change. If a committee member proposes a new direction, someone else will point out the risks. Since few committee members are in a position to carry the load of gathering information and making the case that will overcome opposition, the proposal will likely die.

- Standing committees often foster a sluggish decision-making process. The process of decision making is slow because recommendations are made at monthly committee meetings and require agreement of the members. It will then be up to the board at its monthly meetings to consider the recommendations. This can be particularly problematic if there are urgent issues to consider or time-limited opportunities that could be missed.

3. BOARD AGENDA

Under the traditional governance model, the board's agenda is usually built from four sources. First, there are regular, mandated agenda items such as reading the minutes from the previous board meeting. Second, issues arise from committee minutes and recommendations. Some schools have a third way to get an issue on the board's agenda: by presenting a petition from the constituency that shows there is community support or opposition regarding a particular program or board decision. Sometimes an individual or group may appear to address the board in person. Fourth, issues are brought to the board's attention through the initiative of individual board members. After the regular agenda has been considered, it is common to have roundtable, roll call, or a similarly named process during which each board member can ask questions, make observations, or raise additional issues for the board to consider.

Roundtable has the reputation of generating the greatest emotional debate over issues, partly because the topics are unpredictable. At roundtable, board members may ask the school head about specific cases of student or employee discipline and evaluation. Roundtable is an opportunity for a board member to plead the cause of a parent or teacher seeking review of a previous board or administrative decision, or raise an urgent problem. It is important to point out the problematic practice of roundtable as the board deals impulsively with issues without adequate information.

Consider one example. At the roundtable portion of a board meeting, a board member questions the principal on some students' behavior. The board member relates seeing three boys hunched down, creeping along the outside wall of the school and asks, "Were the boys ditching school or sneaking off to smoke?" The principal responds that he has no idea, but he will check it out and call the board member. The board is left with the impression that the principal got caught being uninformed about the real happenings of the school. The principal calls the board member the next morning: The students were in a math class and were measuring the perimeter of the school building. The teacher was just around the corner, helping other members of the class. If the board member had been genuinely concerned about the children, he could have stopped in the school office or called the school immediately to alert the principal, who then could have intervened. Or the board member could have talked privately with the principal before or after the board meeting. The question did not have to be brought up as a board matter.

If a board member does raise an issue at a roundtable without warning, the principal is unlikely to offer an acceptable explanation on the spot, and is put on the defensive. The question serves only for the board member to appear to say, "I know more about the school than the principal." In this illustration, the explanation is not likely to be clarified for the other board members at the next meeting. Such surprises do not provide valuable information or accountability, nor do they bring improvement. The roundtable process of determining an agenda item allows an individual board member to dominate or manipulate the board's time and topics at the expense of broader issues that the board should be considering.

EVALUATING THE TRADITIONAL GOVERNANCE MODEL

At the end of chapter 2, three pivotal questions were raised that each governance model must address. How are these questions answered under the traditional governance model?

QUESTION 1: How does the school identify and protect its foundational beliefs?

The traditional model does have a number of strengths. For example, the traditional model maintains a direct link between the school and the community or owner. The traditional model does protect and preserve many valued community conventions and practices, and it prevents school leaders from taking risky chances or from following fads. However, the model does have some weaknesses that may affect a school's ability to safeguard foundational beliefs.

The underlying assumption under the traditional model is that the best preserver of the essential theological positions and founding principles of the school is the involvement of a homogeneous community. The community as a whole determines when change should occur.

In many cases, the community is taught to be skeptical of change because change may dilute or remove essential characteristics of the school. The traditional model sometimes does not easily distinguish between traditional practices and foundational beliefs and principles. As community values and goals change, a school may need help in discerning which long-held principles are nonnegotiable and how the school can adapt to a changing constituency without endangering those nonnegotiables.

QUESTION 2: How does the school identify and promote its mission and vision?

Though most schools have a mission statement, some schools operating under the traditional model may have inadequate or ineffective mission statements. The mission statement should drive the school forward toward an ideal. A mission statement that is primarily an attempt to inform the public of the school's general desire or intention will not be enough to guide the school leaders in their decision making. One effect of having an inadequate mission statement is that the school board may be primarily reactive rather than proactive.

The community is often loyal to the school as it was and is, appreciates the school's history and traditions, and sees the school as a very good school. Any problems that are identified by the community are put on the agenda of the standing committees, which make recommendations to the board. However, the board may be reluctant to initiate action. The expectation is that the board's primary role is to be the final filter to protect and preserve the school's essential characteristics. This means that the board may passively wait for problems or recommendations to be placed on its agenda. Few expect such a board to provide leadership by initiating actions or considering opportunities that may enhance the school's ministry and effectiveness. The possibility of establishing a common vision or priority that unites the school community is reduced as each issue is raised and treated separately by different groups rather than as part of a board-controlled plan tied to the school's mission.

There are several symptoms that indicate that the board may be operating mostly by reacting to situations. Here are some of those symptoms:

- The board's own agenda is unpredictable and out of its control. The board agenda is determined by committee reports or roundtable comments. If the board is not setting its own agenda, it certainly is not setting the agenda for the standing committees or for the school as a whole.

- The board addresses problems as isolated events, without considering those issues within a long-range context or an overarching ideal and vision. The board does not regularly engage in long-range strategic planning. This prevents the board from exerting effective leadership toward a common mission.

- Adherents to a particular cause recognize that because there is no standard or written policy, each case is likely to be handled uniquely. This encourages the interested parties to initiate campaigns to persuade receptive board members to take their side. Then the board must discuss such issues in an intense situation under pressure, often without having all of the relevant information.

- Major issues may be discussed, but little action is taken. Because of the limitations and changes connected with the standing-committee approach, the board is rarely in a position to work on issues that take more than one year to accomplish. Sometimes a problem arises for discussion every year, but each time the discussion begins anew and little progress is made toward resolution.

Another potential weakness of a reactive approach to governance is that the board may consider each issue in isolation, without realizing the effects of a decision on the mission of the school as a whole. As an example, consider the effects of such an approach in the area of instruction.

- Teachers may be fairly independent and autonomous in the classroom, with freedom to teach the assigned subjects according to their own interests, timing, and conclusions, as long as there are no major complaints. The textbook series may determine the goals, values, and sequence of what is to be taught. The school may not have a robust vision for a united and integrated curriculum based on a clear founding philosophical position.

- Without a comprehensive philosophy of instruction, administrators often default to one of two strategies for determining the school's curriculum. (1) One strategy is to purchase an already established "Christian" curriculum—at least what appears to be Christian because it provides Bible verses as proof texts. The teachers follow the textbook's table of contents to determine the course outline. With this approach, the Christian school acknowledges that the purchased curriculum has few theological objections. However, the school rarely analyzes the philosophical and worldview implications or the pedagogy assumed by the series. In this case, the school's curriculum is determined by the textbook company rather than being an extension of the school's philosophy. With this strategy for developing curriculum, classroom instruction may not be directly linked to the school's stated mission. (2) Another strategy is simply to trust the individual Christian teachers to bring a Christian educational experience. The school assumes that since the teacher is a Christian, the instruction and classroom activities will promote student learning that is in accord with the school's mission. While the curriculum may not distinctly reflect a Christian perspective, the administration hopes the teacher will add a few appropriate modifications that will encourage the development of Christian ethics and character.

- There are two problems with these strategies. The first problem is that they do not provide a comprehensive, interrelated curriculum that joins the various subjects together with common themes and language. The second problem is that no one is really confident that the curriculum is consistent with the school's philosophy and mission. Giving the teacher complete autonomy in the classroom makes it very difficult for the curriculum to be consistent from year to year. This circumstance is exacerbated if there is a turnover of teachers. It is almost impossible to ensure that the curricular material has continuity with what was taught the previous year and what will be taught the following year. There will likely be duplication and significant gaping holes. This will have a negative year-to-year impact on the students.

QUESTION 3: How does the school identify the roles of authority, determine the process for decision making, and ensure accountability?

Under the traditional model, the school may be vulnerable in several areas.

A. Roles and authority may be unclear. For example, the relationship between the owner and the school board is often undefined, as is the relationship between the board and the school head.

- When a school is owned by a church or diocese, some unique issues related to decision making may arise. It is not uncommon for the church to consider the school board as an advisory body to the church board. As the owner, the church may suddenly intervene in or overturn board decisions. Examples include appointing a new head of school, countermanding board actions, or even closing the school—often without consultation with the school board. Sometimes the church will appoint an individual person (such as a pastor, bishop, attorney, or business manager) to represent the owner. This person often has authority to make decisions regarding any aspect of the school at any time with or without school board approval.

- An association-owned school may also experience problems if there are unclear policies regarding membership and assigned authority. In such schools, board meetings with association members may take place only once or twice per year. Most meetings are routine, but occasionally there may be a controversial issue that is emotionally charged. The owner, parents, or others may demand that they—not the board—make the decision. It is not uncommon for schools to even allow new issues to be raised from the floor of the meeting for association consideration, such as proposing an alternate board candidate or reconsidering a previously made board decision. When there are controversial issues and there are no clear policies of membership and assigned authority, there is often debate as to who is authorized to make the final decision. Often the well-intentioned leaders think that undefined roles will facilitate consensus and symbolize trust. If cordial relationships exist between the owner and the school board, this may not be an obvious issue. But many times the result of imprecise roles is confusion, factions, discontent, mistrust, and high emotion. An assumption of good will is not an adequate safeguard against such situations.

B. Board decisions often are inconsistent and suspiciously interpreted as based on personal relationships. Under the traditional model, previous board decisions may be at best guidelines; they are not policies to serve as a standard for consistency. Because of the focus on specific current issues, each decision is considered as an isolated event, with little regard for the fact that it may be setting a precedent for future decisions. The board should be aware that any decision will be remembered by someone affected by a similar issue, and that person will consider the previous decision to be a precedent of sorts. In today's culture, inconsistent decisions may make the school vulnerable to a wrongful-act lawsuit.

C. The board's style may become adversarial and political. Under the traditional model, the decision-making process, even at the board level, can set up an adversarial structure in which the board's time and energies are spent dealing with competing complaints. The traditional model often has a win/lose culture.

- When the board interacts with the owner through a representative, the representative sees the owner as having primary importance. The representative's responsibility is to review the school board's decisions and directions as they may affect the owner. The representative may be on the lookout for adversarial situations and may see the school programs and priorities as being in competition with the owner. This also means that there could be areas of conflict of interest between the school and the owner. The representative is obligated to do what is perceived to be to the owner's advantage, not necessarily what is in the best interests of the school.

- When the board is not clearly seeking to advance a mission or accomplish a comprehensive goal, the alternative is to look for problems to solve. If there are no obvious problems to address, perhaps it is because the administration is hiding some weak spot. Some board members may see themselves as adversaries of the school head and principals, assuming that the school head deliberately puts a positive spin on circumstances to artificially overstate his or her success, to defend his or her actions, and to hide problems and minimize the negative aspects of the school. The board may think its task is to expose the dirt or to point out additional problems that need to be identified and corrected. These board members think their job is to keep the administrators honest by challenging every administrative action.

D. Under the traditional model, it often is assumed that individual board members have special authority at all times. An individual board member may direct a member of the custodial staff to clean up the trash from an area or to paint a room. While this is well-intentioned and the matter may need attention, such action by a board member can have harmful consequences. It is unlikely that the board member has enough of a grasp of school management details to understand the consequences of that action. A more serious consequence is that the board member's action changes the relationship between employees and the head of school, potentially undermining the head of school's authority, creating an atmosphere of suspicion, and bringing conflict rather than resolution. Employees are asked to respond without having to consult, communicate with, or work through the school head; both the employee and the administrator must guess who is accountable to whom. This tends to cultivate an expectation that board members will listen to and handle complaints outside the organizational structure. When employees have direct access to a board member, it becomes impossible for there to be real trust, cooperation, or accountability among the school's leaders.

E. Under the traditional model, the process of selecting new board members is sometimes treated almost casually. Here is a humorous but unfortunately true example. A person tried to convince a potential board candidate to assent to be on the ballot two days before the owner meeting, with this enticing appeal: "We have asked everybody we can think of to run, but they said no. We already have scraped the bottom of the barrel, and so now we are asking you to serve."

- Under the traditional model, there are three common approaches to choosing board candidates. (1) Choose candidates from family and friends. (2) Choose people who have done the most complaining, in hopes that once they are on the board they will recognize that the board is doing the best it can. (3) A third, very disconcerting strategy is to pick candidates almost at random, or to recommend someone just because the person is willing to serve. If you have experienced board selection discussions under the traditional model, you may have heard something like this: "I don't know who he is, but he seems to be a nice guy. I think he may be an engineer. I see him at most of the basketball games, so he seems to support the school." Since no one on the present board really knows the potential candidate and there don't appear to be any objections, the decision is, "We'll let the owner association determine whether he's the right person."

- In such cases, those interested in serving on a reactionary board are likely to be the problem identifiers and complainers. People known to be leaders or visionaries tend to decline.

F. There may be remarkably little accountability.

- If the school depends too heavily on standing committees, there is no individual hero and no one person to blame if anything goes wrong. When evaluating committee and board decisions, there is no one to hold accountable for poor actions or results—no one to fire, discipline, or retrain. Suppose students are failing standardized academic tests. Whose job would be on the line? The board can't fire the chair of the education standing committee; that person probably is a board member and might be off the board next year. The board can't fire the teachers or community members for their participation; committee work isn't their professional job, and they were only a small part of the relevant decisions.

- There also may be little accountability of the school head. The school head is often more of a manager than a leader. The school board or a standing committee may be given the authority to make decisions on individual problems that arise; the school head is then assigned to carry out the directions. There is confusion regarding relationships between the school board, committees, and school head. While the head of school may have a job description, there is likely no clear way to fire a school head based on poor job performance. The head of school deflects accountability by noting that a standing committee and the board made the decisions; the head of school likely didn't even have a vote, but was merely the manager who implemented the decisions. Thus, dismissal of a head of school is more likely to be for personal reasons, for legal or moral transgressions, or for having poor relations with the board or staff. These may become the official reason for seeking a new school head who can better solve the school's problems. No individual is ultimately accountable for any decisions or actions.

In summary, the traditional model of governance has served Christian school communities for generations—in many cases well. During times of change, however, the inadequacies of the model may become apparent. When unstable circumstances jeopardize the school, school leadership may look for an alternative governance model. The governance-by-policy model is becoming well known as an alternative, and it will be considered next.

FOR REFLECTION AND DISCUSSION

1. What do you think are the advantages and disadvantages of the traditional model of school governance?

2. Discuss the answers to each of the three critical questions. Would you modify or add to the answers given in this chapter?

3. What further questions or concerns do you have about the traditional governance model?

CHAPTER 4

Characteristics of the Governance-by-Policy Model

There are various governance-by-policies models, but probably the most well-known and influential is the model proposed by John Carver (Carver 1997). (Note: There are a number of variations on the Carver model, and there are other governance-by-policy models; however, for brevity this book will refer to *the* governance-by-policy model, referring to a broad governance model rather than a specific variation of the model.) By adopting the governance-by-policy model, many schools have found improved performance and relief from various areas of stress. There are many things to appreciate about the governance-by-policy model, such as limiting the number of committees, creating more accountability, and freeing the school head as CEO to accomplish known board goals within board-defined limits. This allows the school head to collaborate and work with staff to accomplish the goals. The governance-by-policy model is designed to bring accepted corporate business practices to nonprofit organizations. This model will be examined as it relates to Christian schools.

FEATURES OF THE GOVERNANCE-BY-POLICY MODEL

The governance-by-policy model deliberately gives the board the authority to adjust quickly to changing circumstances and to hold the CEO accountable. It will be helpful to consider four business practices that differentiate the governance-by-policy model from the traditional model.

1. THE SCHOOL BOARD MEMBERS OPERATE AS TRUSTEES.

The governance-by-policy model looks for board members to serve as trustees who are concerned about the entire organization. This is in contrast to board members who are representatives of a particular segment of the school constituency (e.g., a supporting church, high school parents, students with special needs, parents seeking high academic results, or families who are struggling financially). Such board members tend to support the interests of that group. Such a representative situation could be planned or may be just a mind-set of individual board members.

The goal of the governance-by-policy model is to free the board from group politics and to have it composed of qualified, committed people who are willing to serve as trustees of the whole school. As a trustee, each board member must have a sense of responsibility for the well-being of the whole organization and must be aware of how departments and issues are related and integrated and how they affect each other.

2. THE BOARD GOVERNS BY POLICIES.

Under the governance-by-policy model the school board writes policies to be followed by itself and policies to be followed by the school head. This resolves much of the confusion coming from operating in reaction to events, as is often found with the traditional model.

3. THE SCHOOL BOARD IS AUTONOMOUS.

For the governance-by-policy model, the best board members should be business savvy and willing to take calculated risks. It is important that board members be trained to deal with the complex tools—for example, balance sheets and income statements—that the board needs to make big-picture decisions.

Parents are understandably focused on their children's success in school. The traditional model may produce situations in which parents lobby board members for decisions the parents think would benefit their children. Political maneuvering can undermine the workings of the board and the effectiveness of the school. The governance-by-policy model is designed to avoid such political intrigue and pressure by making the board autonomous and independent from the general constituency. Under the governance-by-policy model, decisions are likely to be made more professionally and consistently, removing the appearance that things get done based on personal or political influence.

Under the governance-by-policy model the board is the final authority on all issues related to the organization. There is no further appeal. The board, in effect, owns the school. The board's autonomy allows it to change the direction of the organization and to respond to emergencies and unexpected economic or social challenges or opportunities. This also allows the board to act quickly to benefit from unique opportunities that may be available only for a short time, such as purchasing a certain property at a desirable price.

This flexibility allows the board to respond quickly and decisively without having to form a committee or call for special meetings.

4. THE BOARD IS SELF-PERPETUATING.

Since successful board members have a better idea of what qualifications a new board member must possess, it makes sense that the professional board should select its own members in the future. Therefore, the board is authorized to appoint new board members. The board makes its own policies regarding the selection of board members and the length of their terms of office.

EVALUATING THE GOVERNANCE-BY-POLICY MODEL

How are the three critical questions answered under the governance-by-policy model?

QUESTION 1: How does the school identify and protect its foundational beliefs?

The school board has the authority to govern every aspect of the school. The board is self-perpetuating and is independent from the community, so it can concentrate on long-range issues and operate free from public caprice. Board autonomy empowers the board to determine and pursue the goals and philosophy that it thinks will be most effective for the school. The self-governing board is empowered to change the very structure and direction of the school. Under the governance-by-policy model the school's mission and all operations are board-only policies. The board has the authority to determine any nonnegotiables. With such a board, there is some risk that the school may be allowed to drift from its founding commitments. The school should analyze the degree of risk when considering adopting this governance model.

QUESTION 2: How does the school identify and promote its mission and vision?

Every for-profit business and every nonprofit organization, including the Christian school, hopes to meet customer needs and expectations. Most Christian schools do consider consumer demand and make accommodations, but not at the expense of the mission and core philosophical principles. In contrast, for-profit businesses more likely seek to use customer satisfaction as the compass in shaping their products and services. One can easily imagine that when a Christian school board seeks to govern by business practices, it could wander into making decisions based on the premise that customer demands have higher value than maintaining philosophical integrity and consistency.

Members of school boards and school heads operating under the governance-by-policy model soon become aware that applying for-profit operating principles to a nonprofit organization may miss the peculiarities of faith-based nonprofits. Even more critical is that the governance-by-policy literature misses the distinctive organizational features of the Christian school as an educational institution. There are many insights to learn from for-profit businesses, but not all those principles apply to Christian schools.

Not all businesses and nonprofits should be governed the same way. Every organization has unique characteristics that should shape how it structures its governance model and business operations. There are characteristics of culture and practice associated with educational institutions—and specifically Christian schools—that may be different from characteristics of other nonprofits. Ignoring these differences can produce effects that are unproductive and that can even be dangerous to the school's mission.

The Christian school uniquely cultivates learning in children, has a partnership with parents, and purposefully promotes its faith positions. There is an intensity of feeling and commitment that is not likely to be found in any other institution. Leaders cannot merely direct the school by following customer preferences. Parents are placing their precious children in the school's care for the most important purpose in life—to nurture and instruct their children to walk and grow in faith and in relationship to Jesus Christ. Parents prove to be intense advocates for their children.

School leaders may have unrealistic expectations of measurement goals if they do not understand the complexity of what the school or teacher is able or unable to control. Many factors that contribute to the development of the student are outside the control of the school. The home, church, society, peer group, media, and the individual student all have an impact, and the Holy Spirit works in the heart of the student to bring real-life change. All these factors require the school to vigilantly guard and aggressively communicate its mission and vision.

QUESTION 3: How does the school identify the roles of authority, determine the process for decision making, and ensure accountability?

The governance-by-policy model has significant advantages over the traditional model in the decision-making process. It is very helpful to the Christian school if board members serve as trustees rather than representatives. Every board member is then looking out for the success of the whole school, not just reacting to specific interests. It is also helpful for the board to govern by written expectations and policies. These policies can result in predictable and consistent processes, effective measurement, and accountability. The governance-by-policy model also provides an orderly and predictable way to handle issues. The board now defines what decisions it is to make, considers the context and long-range implications, and responds with more consistency in handling similar issues.

While the board of the Christian school desires to have a school that is respected and has financial stability, the board should recognize that the sustainability of the school is not the end of its responsibility. The board of the Christian school seeks to make the school an instrument of Christ's kingdom by nurturing students who will be committed and effective disciples of Jesus Christ as they exhibit vision, understanding, discernment, and service.

ORGANIZATIONAL MISSION DRIFT IN ACTION

How and why did Ivy League universities such as Harvard and Princeton drift from their theological and philosophical moorings? They began as institutions established to produce ministers and an educated Christian community. How could they have gone from promoting the gospel of Jesus Christ to limiting or merely tolerating the Christian message? While the reasons for the changes are complex, there are some key factors to consider.

One factor is that these schools limited the definition of their foundational beliefs to theological doctrines rather than a broader philosophical view. Rarely are the first salvos of challenge a direct assault on the theological positions. The real pressures come from the desire to change a practical issue that has philosophical implications. Consider the illustration of Princeton.

The first compromise was to place learning in a separate compartment from the Scriptures and a Christian worldview. James H. Thornwell, the leading Southern Presbyterians theologian, articulated a long-standing Presbyterian distinction between the covenant of grace, concerning God's offer of salvation, and the covenant of nature, which established God's moral law for nations. To Southern Presbyterians, who were resisting ecclesiastical pronouncements against slavery, this distinction meant that the church should confine itself to matters concerning the covenant of grace and not meddle in matters of the state. The state was bound by God's moral law contained in the covenant of nature, and nations would not be blessed if they did not obey it. Woodrow Wilson held broadly the same view. For Wilson, who emerged as a professional academic during an era when many intellectuals underwent a severe crisis of faith, one use of this distinction was to keep his particular Presbyterian faith and his broader moral categories in more-or-less separate compartments in his scholarship (Marsden 1994, 224–25).

The second compromise was to place these compartments under different authorities. The Bible was relegated to address doctrinal issues appropriate for the church, while the "real world" would be guided by science, which was considered to be neutral. In the Princeton University story, the alternative to a biblical worldview was modernism and a reliance on science to provide the answers for life. Soon science was given the authority to determine what parts of the Bible were authentic and how to interpret them. The ultimate question was one of authority. In the previous generation science and Scripture had been, in effect, coequal authorities. Now science was declared the highest authority (Marsden 1994, 20).

Although the university was broadly Christian, its higher commitments were to scientific and professional ideals and to demands for a unified public life; therefore, academic expressions of Christianity seemed at best superfluous and at worst unscientific and unprofessional. Most of those associated with higher education were still Christians, but in academic life, as in other parts of modern life, religion increasingly was confined to private spheres (Marsden 1994, 263).

Note that the university did not change its theological stance. Rather, it changed philosophical priorities, which allowed for a more direct challenge to the foundational position of the institution. The board had no accountability for preserving the foundational faith position when hiring faculty or determining curriculum. The school would hire a professor of academic renown even though the board knew the person did not share the school's founding faith commitment:

> As President [of Princeton University], Wilson essentially toned down the religious emphasis that had prevailed under the [previous Princeton University President] Patton regime…The impetus for Wilson's resolution of the Patton problem as well as in terminating the Sunday afternoon service was apparently the desire to eliminate Presbyterian dogmatism from the curriculum. He also signaled the end of religious tests for the faculty by hiring the first Jew to teach at Princeton in 1904 and the first Roman Catholic in 1909. In 1906 he had the university formally declared nonsectarian. (Marsden 1994, 227)

The issue was not overcoming anti-Semitism or a bias against Roman Catholics; rather, the school board changed the founding Presbyterian doctrinal and worldview beliefs without needing permission from any other authority. This path led to being nonsectarian and to a conscious abandoning of the school's founding principles.

Other American universities provide examples of the same separation from their religious roots because the board was unaccountable for holding these faith positions.

FOR REFLECTION AND DISCUSSION

1. What do you think are the advantages and disadvantages of the governance-by-policy model?

2. Discuss the governance-by-policy answers to each of the three critical questions. Would you modify or add to the answers given in this chapter?

3. What questions or concerns do you have about the governance-by-policy model?

CHAPTER 5

Characteristics of the Mission-Directed Governance Model

The mission-directed governance model endeavors to incorporate the best of both the traditional and governance-by-policy models. Under the traditional model there is a close relationship between the board, the owner, and the school community, and the board is expected to govern in light of the core beliefs and values of the community. On the other hand, the Christian school can learn much from the governance-by-policy model, especially with regard to processes and operations, the expectation of measurement, and holding the school head accountable.

For some Christian schools under the traditional model, foundational philosophical principles are not articulated in the governing documents; the school operates under the assumption that a homogeneous school community will keep the school rooted in its founding principles. The result may be that the school constituents develop an aversion toward any type of change, even in nonessential issues.

An unspoken assumption with the traditional model is that everyone who remains in the homogeneous community will forever know and support the foundational beliefs. Under the governance-by-policy model the school relies on the integrity of the present board members to ensure that future boards will always adhere to the founding principles. Both assumptions can be dangerous in a changing community.

The mission-directed governance model is designed to avoid such dangers. It embraces and incorporates the view that the school board should govern by policies and that the board members should serve as trustees rather than as representatives. However, the mission-directed approach aims to both protect the essential philosophical foundations of the school and to promote progress toward an ideal. It is intended to advance the cause of Christian education using contemporary business tools. The challenge of the mission-directed governance model will be to inseparably fuse the actions of the board to the school's philosophy and mission, preserve the essential beliefs, and promote the integration of learning with faith positions.

FEATURES OF THE MISSION-DIRECTED MODEL

The foundational assumptions of the governance model produce corresponding expectations, attitudes, behaviors, and results. This governance model has the following characteristics.

1. THE MISSION DRIVES EVERYTHING.

The phrase *education on purpose* describes the Christian school that follows the mission-directed governance model. Agreement of the owner, board, administration, and faculty on the school's mission brings opportunity for unity, vision, and accountability. There will be more community support as the school's goals and priorities are focused and consistent. There will be more optimism as the school emphasizes what is to be accomplished instead of what went wrong. Education on purpose brings clearer expectations, understood criteria for accountability, and focused decision making. The school community's understanding of the school's purpose brings attention and passion to student learning.

The mission-directed Christian school must have a clear understanding of its biblical mandate so that school leadership can take responsibility for leading the school toward a clear target. To define the purpose of education, the mission-directed school should have a written philosophy and mission that enable the school to clarify and solidify its beliefs, ideals, and intentions. This allows the school community to more effectively identify its foundational positions and consequently preserve and protect these principles. These foundational positions that the school resolves not to change are the school's *nonnegotiables*.

If the philosophy and mission are not given written articulation, but merely left as assumed principles with multiple interpretations, it is difficult or impossible to achieve meaningful philosophical ends.

2. THE SCHOOL STRIVES TO REACH AN IDEAL.

Under the mission-directed governance model, a clearly defined purpose of education is articulated in the school's mission statement. The board, as the unified central authority, has the responsibility to initiate change that leads the students to fulfill that purpose—to grow in becoming the kind of followers of Jesus called for in Scripture.

The Christian school must be committed to pursuing its ideal. School improvement is more than solving current problems. The mission-directed governance model emphasizes that the ideal is still out there and is a target toward which the school must continue to strive. The mission-directed model begins with the assumption that the school model will not be perfect even if immediate problems can be solved.

Problems must be addressed, but if the board merely concentrates on solving problems, everyone knows those problems will soon be replaced by other problems. The mission-directed model seeks not merely to deal with immediate problems but to prevent problems from appearing—by working to reach the goal of what the school ought to become. When the board focuses on making the ideal real and effective, many problems can be avoided.

Acknowledging that there is room to create new ways to achieve student learning allows the board to initiate proactive change that will help the school advance toward its ideal and challenge the status quo. For example, the board may decide that to achieve its mission, students should be involved in service or missions projects or the curriculum must include a course or unit on Christian leadership.

Under the mission-directed governance model, the board believes that the school is living in the "silver" age. The board will work hard toward the ideal so that future generations may build upon what is done today. Perhaps the "gold" and even the "platinum" ages of the school are still to come. This mind-set allows the school to respect and celebrate what others have believed and done in the past without seeking to nostalgically go back to former times. The school board sees itself in the process of more firmly establishing and integrating the essential beliefs while reforming and transforming the ministry to address present circumstances and future possibilities.

3. THE WHOLE ORGANIZATION IS ALIGNED WITH THE MISSION.

Mission-directed governance establishes a structure that encourages the board to ensure that every feature and program of the organization aligns with and positively reflects the mission. Governance should be more than providing a way to have an orderly board meeting and a predictable process for making decisions. The board's role must be more than simply managing finances, raising funds, building and upgrading facilities, and establishing the organizational image. Under the mission-directed governance model, the board is given a mandate to bring every aspect of the school into alignment with the mission. This includes board guardianship of student learning and curriculum, extracurricular activities, auxiliary organizations, and decisions regarding admissions, employment, student discipline, and all other critical aspects of the school. The board guides these areas by mission-linked policy rather than by direct involvement.

4. THE BOARD IS LINKED TO THE COMMUNITY.

As with the governance-by-policy model, the mission-directed model frees the board from many of the personal and political pressures associated with the traditional model. It requires that the board maintain the integrity of the school's philosophy, without resisting all change.

The mission-directed model sees the ties to the owner as one of the best characteristics of the traditional model. The purpose of the board is to lead the school community in achieving its philosophical and mission mandate. At the same time, it outlines specific limits to the owner's involvement and identifies the means by which the owner will continue to hold the board accountable for providing leadership.

The mission-directed governance model recommends that the board not be directly involved in daily decision making; the board does not need to know everything that is happening at the school. The board will communicate regularly and listen to the constituency, but with the purpose of discovering what is needed to help form the vision and long-range goals and come closer to the ideal—not to resolve personal complaints The board members act as trustees; they serve the entire school community and do not serve as representatives of special-interest groups.

5. THE SCHOOL MAKES DECISIONS AS A UNIFIED COMMUNITY, NOT JUST AS A COLLECTION OF INDIVIDUALS.

The school community, the owner, and the school administrators recognize that the school belongs to Jesus Christ and that they are mere stewards. The community achieves unity by adherence to and promotion of the ideals communicated by the mission and philosophy rather than by geographic proximity, family ancestry, history, ethnicity, denominational affiliation, or other circumstantial criteria. This perspective offers a secure and nondiscriminatory way for a new family to become part of the decision-making community. All members must exhibit understanding of and commitment to the school's philosophy and mission. Even if the vision and strategies must occasionally change to meet changing cultural realities, such changes are made in partnership with the owner and the school board.

This does not mean that everyone is involved in every decision, but there is agreement on the purpose and direction of the school. The owner, the school board, the administration, the faculty, and the constituency together promote and expand the ideals for which the school stands. The roles of each element are defined with delegated powers and specified limitations.

6. THE SCHOOL BOARD ESTABLISHES AN ORGANIZED, EFFICIENT PROCESS OF OPERATION COVERING DECISION MAKING, ROLES, AUTHORITY, MEANS OF MEASUREMENT, AND ACCOUNTABILITY.

When changes are necessary, the school needs a clear process that matches the role and authority of the decision makers to the depth and range of the issue to be resolved. Change should not be based on impulse, on public opinion, or on pressure from influential community members.

Under the mission-directed governance model, the board determines goals and priorities, gives oversight, and holds others accountable for achieving the goals. The board will govern by written policies that give direction regarding how to achieve those goals. The board hires and gives authority to the head of school as the chief executive officer to ensure that all aspects of the school comply with the board policies and directives. The roles of authority and action between board and CEO are clearly distinguished and separated.

By taking a proactive philosophical position, the mission-directed governance model seeks to unite all aspects of the school to its educational philosophy. The board takes on the responsibility of providing this leadership by

- establishing policies that define the purposes and content of curricular and extracurricular programs;
- establishing policies to give direction for school operations so that the school will be a living example of a Christian school;
- giving the school head the authority, direction, and tools to establish practices relating to admissions, student life, discipline, employee

hiring and benefits, employee evaluation, and all other aspects of the school; and

- ensuring that the school head is accountable for accomplishing the board directions by requiring the school head to submit reports, by conducting surveys, and by consulting outside evaluators who can provide financial reviews and audits and confirmations in other areas.

Under the mission-directed board governance model, the board makes decisions as a unit. This places the board in a strong leadership position to guide and control all aspects of the school through the school head. The board defines the target—the ideal for the school—and determines the direction, priority, and pace of the means to reach that target.

The board under the mission-directed model will find itself dealing with more critical items on the agenda than would be possible under the traditional model, with more organization and minimal surprises. It can produce creative solutions because it is not merely reacting to specific individual cases but is able to consider long-range issues. Mission-directed governance brings accountability by giving leadership responsibilities to the head of school. The board practices self-control by refraining from direct involvement and by delegating day-to-day decisions to the head of school. The board can then praise the head of school for accomplishing the task and correct or discipline the head of school if the he or she fails to accomplish the board's directives.

EVALUATING THE MISSION-DIRECTED GOVERNANCE MODEL

How are the three critical questions addressed under the mission-directed governance model?

QUESTION 1: How does the school identify and protect its foundational beliefs?

The school identifies and formally defines its essential beliefs and positions—its nonnegotiables—in the covenant with the owner as well as in board policies. Consequently, both the board and owner clearly know what are the founding positions, and both must approve any change in any of these foundational beliefs.

QUESTION 2: How does the school identify and promote its mission and vision?

The school has a clearly defined mission statement on which both the owner and the board agree. The school board consciously spurs the school to achieve its mission. The board—with the help of the school administration and other constituents—develops a vision for implementing that mission in present and future circumstances. The board evaluates present circumstances, considers the ideal, and determines a plan for accomplishing that ideal.

QUESTION 3: How does the school identify the roles of authority, determine the process for decision making, and ensure accountability?

To provide leadership and accountability, the board establishes policies giving purpose and direction to every aspect of the school. Under the board's leadership, each element of the school community participates according to its identified role and authority. Each person or group has defined purposes, authority, and limitations—which will reduce distractions and promote a community united in striving to be a model Christian school—and brings substantial accountability in following defined, measurable goals.

The school board is positioned to develop a vision, articulate criteria by which to evaluate present programs, and determine the direction and priorities to be promoted. However, it is also critical that the board remove itself from the habit of school management.

FOR REFLECTION AND DISCUSSION

1. What do you think are the advantages and disadvantages of the mission-directed governance model?

2. Discuss the mission-directed-governance answers to each of the three critical questions. How would you modify or add to the answers given in this chapter?

3. What questions or concerns do you have about the mission-directed governance model?

PART TWO

How the Mission-Directed Governance Model Works

CHAPTER 6

Preparing for Education on Purpose

Before looking at the details of how the mission-directed governance model works, it is important for school leaders to take some time to carefully define and clearly articulate what the school is trying to achieve. What is the purpose of the school?

The Christian school needs a clear understanding of its biblical mission and philosophy. The mission statement is a brief description of the purpose the school is committed to achieve. Because the school philosophy describes the rationale for the school, it provides criteria for identifying what should be preserved and protected, and what the school leaders are to promote and enhance. In a broad sense the philosophy will include the kernel of what students are to learn, the ideal toward which the school is aiming, and specific goals for achieving that ideal.

Since the philosophy and the mission statement describe the essential purpose and characteristics of the school, the school leaders must strive to make every aspect of the school a consistent extension of them. The mission and philosophy statements provide stable and consistent criteria for anticipating and managing change by establishing policies and initiating actions; they also place owner, board members, administrators, teachers, and other school leaders on the same side, trying to accomplish the same identified goals.

Providing chapel and Bible courses does not make a school a Christian school. The implications of exalting Jesus as Savior and Lord must saturate every course, policy, and action. Curriculum and learning outcomes should fulfill the school's identified purpose. The school must deliberately design learning goals to equip students to bring relationships, society, and culture under the lordship of Jesus Christ. The mission-directed governance model is designed to align every aspect of the school with the school's stated mission and philosophy.

All school programs and practices should purposefully enhance the school's mission and reflect a balance of priorities with the goal of developing students into whole-life Christian disciples. The school's operation and practices are also an extension of its philosophy and mission, including the governance process itself as well as employee expectations, finances, facilities, communication, student discipline, and even relationships with auxiliary organizations, families, and the government. The school's purpose should be clearly presented in the school's mission statement and philosophy statement; it also should be articulated in its vision statement, slogan, and other official communications.

STATEMENT OF PHILOSOPHY

The philosophy of the school is an extension of the biblical theology, principles, and worldview that motivated the establishment of the school. The philosophy provides the rationale and purpose for education in the school, describes the core unchanging principles upon which the school rests and the ideal toward which the ministry strives, and directs the purpose and practices of the school.

For example, a school's philosophy may declare that the educational program of the school should shape the students' understanding of the relationship between faith and life. What should the school teach students about interaction with society and culture? Should students be taught to retreat, engage, or remain neutral toward society and culture? How should the school relate faith to standard curricular subjects such as reading, writing, mathematics, social studies, art, and music? Are these subjects merely bait to entice students to enroll in the school to hear the story of salvation? Are these subjects to be taught primarily to help the student get a job? Or are the subjects designed to be necessary for discipleship that advances Christ's kingdom by bringing all relationships under the authority of Jesus Christ?

School leaders must know the school's theological and philosophical position in order to understand the purpose and motivation for its ministry. The board should write a short (one or two pages) statement of philosophy. The statement of philosophy should be brief enough for familiarity and readability, but lengthy enough to explain the motivation and vision for the school.

This chapter includes sample philosophy and mission statements that describe a purposeful Christian education in which all aspects of the school, including student learning, are to align with the philosophy and mission. The school's goal is "whole-life discipleship": that every student will follow Jesus Christ as Savior and Lord. The school leaders write the school's own unique philosophy. (Each school's philosophy will reflect the uniqueness of that school; the one provided here is merely one example.)

SAMPLE PHILOSOPHY STATEMENT

The _____ Christian School is a necessary and joyful means to bring glory and honor to God in response to His mercy to His people. The school is necessary because education is essential for effective obedience to God's will; it is joyful because as God's children we individually and communally serve, explore, participate, and delight in His creation.

Every human being has a faith-based perspective or worldview that directs and empowers the way he or she speaks, acts, and lives. The educational perspective of the _____ Christian School is based on the authority of the Bible as the written Word of God. This school recognizes that Christians adhere to a variety of confessional standards, and it actively supports an interdenominational ministry by helping all parents in their efforts to lead their children in the nurture and admonition of the Lord.

One way to summarize the philosophy of this school is to understand the relationships between the individual and God, the individual and self, the individual and other human beings, and the individual and all other aspects of God's creation. The purpose of this school is to train the students to live in and respond to these relationships in accordance with God's Word.

In creation these relationships were established to bring honor and glory to God. Human beings, created in the image of God, were given a special responsibility to be God's representatives to ensure that their life and all of their relationships were consistent with the ideals God had established. People were given special roles as stewards of the earth.

All of the ideal relationships, however, were distorted when human beings willfully rejected their original relationship to God and attempted to build their own kingdom. In spite of humanity's response, God provided through the atonement of Jesus Christ the means of restoring this relationship. As God acts to restore His relationship with human beings, this permits the restoration of each of the other relationships. In thankful response, men and women are free to serve God as sovereign Lord, to love and respect themselves as God's image-bearers, to love their neighbors, and to subdue, control, and preserve the earth as God's stewards.

As Christians we are called to grow in maturity in Jesus Christ, to be knowledgeable about our faith, to spread the gospel of Jesus as Savior and Lord, to stand firm in our convictions, to live as servants in community, and to work toward reconciling all things and relationships to Jesus Christ.

The home has the primary responsibility for the children and is the children's primary source of nurture and guidance. The school serves as an extension of the home. The Christian school encourages the student and family to become part of the body of Christ and urges the family to grow in faith and practice with regular and active involvement in a local Christian congregation.

In the Great Commission, Jesus commands the Christian community to go and make disciples, "… teaching them to obey everything I have commanded you" (Matthew 28:20). Sharing the gospel certainly means telling the story and reality of Jesus as Savior. It also means ensuring that students understand that accepting Jesus as Savior entails accepting Jesus as Lord. The goal of the Christian life is to serve God in all relationships. The student is to learn the skills needed to take responsibility for self, family, church, community, and vocation. The purpose of discipleship education is to equip the student for works of service (Ephesians 4:12). In order to take responsibility for their potential areas of service, the students need each of the curricular subjects.

The school is to help the parents train their children to be mature and unique within the family of God and to accept deliberately and joyfully their special responsibilities. The school is to be an effective instrument of God on behalf of the parents to train their children to become mature followers of Jesus Christ, desirous and capable of developing the relationships established by God.

The school must help the students, as image-bearers of God and members of a faith community, to discover and develop their individual worth, talents, gifts, and responsibilities. The training of students must ensure that every aspect of learning—including vision, understanding, decision making, and serving—is an extension of a Christian commitment and biblical worldview.

1. Vision. The student is to understand who Jesus Christ is and see Him as Savior and Lord. There should be an attitude of awe, worship, and obedience toward God. The student is to understand what it means to be a disciple.

2. Understanding. More than accumulation of knowledge, the student needs a comprehensive understanding of a Christian worldview and its implications in contrast to non-Christian worldview alternatives. The student must know God, self, others, and all of creation. The student must learn what the proper relationships were created to be, what they became through sin, and what they can become through restoration in Jesus Christ. There must be growth in knowledge, in a clear understanding of what things are like, and in differentiation between observations, concepts, and generalizations. There must be growth in ability to analyze, synthesize, apply, create, and interpret.

3. Decision making, discernment, and critical thinking. The school must train and admonish the student to respond appropriately and to apply knowledge in forming relationships as directed in the Bible. There must be growth in right choosing, discernment, appreciation, right attitudes, and the making of appropriate judgments and commitments. The student needs to grow in critical thinking, perspicacity, and wisdom.

4. Service and application. The school must train the student how to act, respond, and apply biblical principles in establishing God-glorifying relationships. In order to promote a positive impact in the world, there must be vision, conviction, and an ability to implement these biblical principles. The student needs to be equipped for doing works of service and for bringing justice and righteousness to the community. The school should provide experiences and opportunities for students to serve and to actually apply those skills to real situations.

SCHOOL VISION, THEME, SLOGAN, AND MOTTO

THE MANDATE FOR VISION

It is important to remember that the board, church, or association does not ultimately own the school. The school is Christ's school. The owner, board, administration, faculty, and staff are stewards of what the Lord is entrusting to them. The school leaders are responsible to build the school in ways that will best build the kingdom of Jesus Christ. They will be held accountable for their stewardship, not only when Christ comes again, but also in the present. Christ gave several sermons and parables on stewardship. One is the parable of the talents (Matthew 25:14–30), in which the steward who only preserved the talent was unfaithful; the stewards who invested their talents, took appropriate risks, and brought the yield were called good and faithful. Other passages call God's people to pursue an ideal:

> Not that I have already obtained all this, or have already arrived at my goal, but I press on to take hold of that for which Christ Jesus took hold of me. Brothers and sisters, I do not consider myself yet to have taken hold of it. But one thing I do: Forgetting what is behind and straining toward what is ahead, I press on toward the goal to win the prize for which God has called me heavenward in Christ Jesus. (Phil. 3:12–14)

> Be very careful, then, how you live—not as unwise but as wise, making the most of every opportunity, because the days are evil. (Eph. 5:15–16)

> You are the light of the world. A town built on a hill cannot be hidden. Neither do people light a lamp and put it under a bowl. Instead they put it on its stand, and it gives light to everyone in the house. In the same way, let your light shine before others, that they may see your good deeds and glorify your Father in heaven. (Matt. 5:14–16)

The school needs to initiate appropriate change—change that makes progress toward an agreed-upon goal.

CONCEPTS IDENTIFYING DIRECTION

Vision is an integral element to advancing the mission; it is not optional. Without vision, the school will settle into preserving the status quo, revert to problem solving, and use the mission as only a theme. Without vision, the governance model becomes merely a process for maintaining order.

Vision is an imprecise term, describing what is not yet but could be. In this book, *vision* refers to an image of the ideal student and of the characteristics of an ideal school. It also will refer to the myriad of ideas and concepts that could help bring about the ideal.

Vision can be on the scale of the big picture and grand design, or it can be on the level of coming up with a particular idea of how to tackle some job in a better way. The early vision for establishing a school probably came as a big-picture idea that some individual, group, or church introduced even before a mission statement was written. Such a big-picture discussion of the vision of the school probably began with passionate conversations regarding the philosophical and practical reasons for founding the school. The leaders shared their aspirations and hopes as they imagined what the results in the lives of their children would be. In this sense, vision provided the big picture of what this ministry could accomplish.

As the school develops, vision may involve imagining the ideal student and identifying the characteristics of a school that will nurture such a student. Vision provides the broad unifying force for developing strategies that accomplish the mission. School leaders must ensure that they not only have ideas for change, but that they have vision to give ideas a context. Making time for opportunities to envision and brainstorm can give rise to meaningful programs, changes in curriculum, educational experiences, and improvement in communication and esprit de corps. These vision ideas lead to a course of action that will contribute to carrying out the school's mission.

Themes and slogans usually have an intended short life span to call attention to a particular project or goal. Schools often announce themes for chapel that may guide devotions. Fund-raising campaigns usually have a slogan to draw attention to some purpose such as tuition assistance or a new playground. Such themes are usually designed to have a limited life.

School mottoes are designed to be more permanent phrases that provide a concise summary of the mission and intentionally draw attention to the heart of the mission. For example, schools may have a catchphrase on school stationery such as "Teaching the whole child," "All for Christ," "Developing Christian character," or "Developing the Christian mind." As inspiring as such mottoes may be, they don't necessarily drive the content of the curriculum or shape the policies that guide school operations.

MISSION STATEMENT

The mission statement turns the philosophical position and visionary aspirations into an identifiable objective that the community is committed to achieving. The mission statement clearly defines the school's purpose in terms of whom it intends to serve and why. This mission statement should unify and align all aspects of the school to accomplish a defined purpose. The school's curriculum and operations are designed to conform to and extend the mission in order to cultivate the ideal student.

There is a common misconception about a mission statement. Too many consider the mission statement to be merely for promotion and marketing. The result is that mission statements are often poorly written and may contain meaningless platitudes or sentimental slogans. Such mission statements are not measurable and don't distinguish the kinds of programs the school will use to accomplish the mission. Such statements are more appropriate for a theme or motto than for a mission statement.

The mission statement should drive and focus organizational expectations, operations, procedures, and facilities toward accomplishing the mission and guiding school culture. The mission should provide criteria to determine what information the board needs in order to lead, as well as provide tools for evaluation and direction for strategic planning—and consequently, criteria for determining priorities, budget, and resources needed for the school to advance toward accomplishing the mission.

A clear and focused mission makes possible more effective communication between the board, the owner, and the faculty. The mission statement guides the school leadership to initiate goals and actions that will achieve the school's mission. The mission statement provides criteria by which school leadership can determine what programs and services to provide as well as criteria for evaluating them. The mission statement articulates the school's purpose and is designed to provide actual goals for student learning that will influence formation of the curriculum and the school's practices.

The school leaders can take responsibility for bringing meaningful change toward a clear mission with vision, unity, and accountability. However, the school needs a clear idea of the target or else the leaders may be diverted from the mission to pursue impulsive fads or merely fix complaints.

A well-crafted mission statement provides the best possibility of bringing unity because the board, administration, faculty, and constituents agree on what is the purpose of the ministry and have an understanding of what "ought to be."

To form a good mission statement, the school leaders need to clearly identify what the Christian school is trying to accomplish. Why does the school exist? Why should parents send their children to this Christian school? Why should church leaders recommend it? Why should donors contribute to its success? What would attract highly qualified faculty and staff to join this ministry?

It is difficult to write an effective mission statement because it must distill the essence of the whole theology and philosophy of the school into a few sentences—and also include as many specific points as possible. School leaders will establish policies that explain and mandate more details. The school leaders will want to use the mission statement to establish curriculum, programs, and policies that are designed to cultivate the growth of each student. The school leadership will want to use the concepts to determine what programs and services to provide as well as criteria for measuring their effectiveness. This statement also provides the basis for accountability.

A well-written mission statement can contribute to the following desirable characteristics:

1. There can be unity regarding the purpose of the school and what it should be accomplishing.

2. The mission statement gives a purpose that pushes the school to align all curriculum, programs, and procedures to accomplish this mandate.

3. A mission that guides the school will influence the school's culture, the motivations of personnel, and the staff's expectations for relationships and practices.

4. The students and all associated with the school should have a clear understanding of their calling, commitment, and purpose of acknowledging Jesus Christ as Savior and Lord.

5. There can be measurement criteria by which to evaluate the school's programs, services, and policies.

6. The school leadership can set goals and make meaningful strategic plans.

7. The school leadership can initiate pointed actions that will advance the mission.

QUESTIONS TO ASK WHEN FORMING A MISSION STATEMENT

The concepts included in the mission statement should be chosen primarily for philosophical reasons, not just because of tradition or current trends.

1. *Why is it important for this school to exist?* State these reasons in a positive manner, expressing what the school is meant to accomplish rather than what the school leaders are against.

2. *What is the ultimate goal of student learning?* How is student learning related to knowing Jesus Christ as Savior and Lord? Why are academic subjects taught?

3. *What population segment is the school trying to serve?* For example, some schools philosophically limit admission to families that are already Christian or from a particular church or background. The mission statement should identify the school's constituents.

4. *How can the school avoid restricting future boards from considering appropriate future opportunities?* The school needs to be careful not to make present circumstances part of the philosophical foundation that can't be changed. Some example could be defining grade levels served, serving a specific location, presently serving as a boarding school, or association with a specific church. While such circumstances may not change, it may be wise to let a future board assess the financial and legal circumstances at that time to determine whether such changes need to be made. Experienced observers know that church pastors and priorities change, local and national economic circumstances change, and facility and technology expectations change.

5. *How can the mission statement maintain balance between being too specific and not being specific enough?* Be aware that the mission statement is meant to encourage education on purpose! The board will make policies that determine goals, measure progress, and determine accountability as guided by the mission statement.

The following is a sample mission statement designed to accomplish a whole-life discipleship education that was introduced in the sample school philosophy.

> The mission of _____ Christian School is to provide and promote a biblically based, quality education that nurtures students to grow in discipleship—equipped with vision, understanding, discernment, and service—in order to renew all relationships and culture to be under the authority of Jesus Christ

This sample mission statement contains central elements that were introduced in the statement of philosophy:

- The name of the school
- The Bible as the foundation
- The purpose— to nurture students to grow in discipleship
- Specific characteristics of discipleship—vision, understanding, discernment, and service
- The statement that the purpose of discipleship education is to instruct and equip students to place all relationships, society, and culture under the authority of Christ
- The statement that the quality of learning can be measured by the degree students master the characteristics that lead to the ideal

If one wonders whether a school is driven to accomplish the mission, the leaders should ask whether the mission is used at budget time. Another relevant indicator is whether the students, teachers, parents, and board members know why they are part of a Christian school and what difference that makes. If your school is educating on purpose, they will be very familiar with the mission statement.

To summarize, the statement of philosophy provides a theoretical rationale for the purpose of education. The mission statement declares the school leaders' determination to provide a particular kind of school for children and young adults to accomplish that philosophical purpose, and it provides the target toward which school leaders aim, with implications for what is to be taught and what programs are to be pursued.

The vision statement will imagine possible approaches to reach the target, motivating engagement with actual ideas and practices to reach the mission. This permits and even encourages change toward a target around which there is a consensus, yet prevents change for change's sake.

A healthy school governance model ensures that the vision and mission give direction to all aspects of the school, including what to teach and how to make the school a living example of a Christian learning community. This also requires the board to know what it must not change.

FOR REFLECTION AND DISCUSSION

1. Describe the difference between a school's philosophy statement, vision statement, and mission statement.

2. What are your observations on the sample philosophy of education?

3. What are your observations on the sample mission statement?

4. What are your observations on having the mission statement serve primarily for internal direction and secondarily for promotion?

CHAPTER 7

Tools to Preserve
and Protect Nonnegotiables

Many Christian educators ask how they can prevent their school from wandering from its founding principles. Sometimes this concern causes suspicion of any change; this can lead to the thinking that maintaining the status quo in all aspects of the school will better protect the founding philosophical positions. At the same time, the school leaders should be able to make changes that contribute to the school's mission. The solution to this quandary is for the school to clearly identify and protect those positions that they are committed to not changing. When the board and constituency know that the faith positions are protected, then they will have greater freedom and less fear as the board initiates needed changes. Having unity on what the school will not change gives more confidence and courage to move toward a new idea. Under the mission-directed governance model, schools clearly identify the positions or characteristics that must not change. These characteristics are called the school's *nonnegotiables*.

How can the school identify its nonnegotiables? Likely nonnegotiables may include that the school will refuse to change its educational model from being founded on the Bible. Examples of other nonnegotiables may include a theological foundation or perspective explained in identified creeds or confessions. Some schools insist that their school is open only to families in which at least one parent is a confessing Christian.

It is important to avoid identifying a position as a nonnegotiable if there is a possibility that circumstances may require the school to change this position. For example, it may not be wise to state as a nonnegotiable that the school will always be part of a particular denomination or congregation. There are too many examples in which future pastors and church boards have different priorities than the school founders. There may be economic circumstances that cause the owner to no longer support the school. Nonnegotiables should not include situations that are outside the control of school leaders. The school may need to remain flexible regarding other aspects of the school, such as school colors, mascot, school nickname, or location.

The mission-directed governance model provides guidelines to help the school protect and preserve its nonnegotiables.

- Nonnegotiables should be identified as such in the covenant between the school board and the owner. The impact of this action is that the board cannot change a nonnegotiable on its own. The nonnegotiable is more than a board policy. Any proposed change to a nonnegotiable will need approval of the owner.

- The board must recommend to the owner only board candidates who agree that they will not seek to change the nonnegotiables.

- Board policies allow the board to remove—by board action alone—any member who attempts to change a nonnegotiable.

Questions to Ask When Determining Nonnegotiables

1. What foundational positions are so essential that the school leaders would consider closing the school if they changed?

2. Are these pivotal positions based on biblical and philosophical principles or on current preferences?

3. How do these positions affect who is served, the essential nature and purpose of Christian education, or the expected results in the lives of students?

4. Are there any situations regarding the organization, owner, association, cultural or historical factors, or other circumstances that should be considered nonnegotiables?

5. As you review the list of possible nonnegotiables, are there circumstances you can envision in which it may be legitimate to consider changing that position?

6. Is the board prepared to dismiss a board member who advocates changing any of the listed nonnegotiables?

COVENANT

The covenant is the agreement between the owner and the school boar The nonnegotiables (as distinct from traditions that the school hopes to preserve but that are not critical to the school's identity) must be put in writing. The school cannot afford to leave the nonnegotiables as assumptions. The nonnegotiables must be included in the covenant with the owner to ensure that they are safely in the control of the owner. The covenant may require that those seeking to become members of the owner group (if the owner is an association) sign a commitment not to change the nonnegotiables as identified in the covenant—usually the statements regarding the mission, the philosophy, and the founding biblical position of the school. Any change to a nonnegotiable must be approved by the owner.

There may be circumstances in which the nonnegotiables must be discussed. Perhaps there is a change in the political situation—such as tax policies or laws that require changes regarding policies for hiring or admissions. There may be some other major change in the community. In such circumstances the board must propose a change and submit the proposal to the owner. The owner has the authority to deny or accept the proposed change.

THE BOARD PROTECTS THE ESSENTIAL FOUNDATIONAL CHARACTERISTICS

As boards consider adopting the mission-directed model of governance, they should note how the foundational purpose and position of the school are protected, especially if the community is no longer homogeneous.

- The board must require that all board members and board candidates support the nonnegotiables.

- Every school board member must sign a code of ethics and commitment as a condition of officially serving on the school board. This code should contain a list of attitudes, behaviors, and positions that each board member must hold. Board candidates are expected to closely review this document before signing it so that any questions or reservations can be considered and discussed before new board members are allowed to take on board responsibilities. The commitments include the essential characteristics of the school, the school's nonnegotiables, and the principles by which the school philosophy will be protected and promoted. The code should include the provision that board members must pledge their support of the nonnegotiables and state their willingness to resign from the board if they can no longer support those nonnegotiables.

- The board should have policies granting it authority and outlining the process for dismissing a member who seeks to change a nonnegotiable and does not voluntarily agree to resign.

- The owner can recall board members. If a board member seeks to change a nonnegotiable, board policies should empower the owner and define the process for removing that board member from office.

The board must recognize its obligation both to preserve the essential characteristics of the school and to promote the school's philosophy. A strong position of promoting and building upon the foundational principles provides a stronger defense than passively guarding theological statements.

POLICIES PROVIDE LEGAL SUPPORT

Having stated policies achieves consistency in practices and limits exposure to political and legal battles. For example, one school that had adopted the mission-directed governance model found itself in a controversy that became the subject of a high-profile media blitz with intense political pressure. The school asked a family to withdraw from the school because the family no longer met the school's requirements for admission. While sensitive details of this case cannot be shared, the school's position was protected because the school had clear policies for admission. Legal advisors declared that the board policy handbook and the admission policy were clearly written and legally sound. The family did not pursue legal recourse, and there were no negative repercussions.

Because such admission restrictions were stated, the process authorized the head of school to carry out the board directives. No separate committee or board meetings were necessary to decide whether such family conditions were acceptable. Without such previously declared policies, the school might have become embroiled in a long, highly visible legal battle that could have ended with the children continuing to be enrolled because there had not been a clearly written agreement to the contrary. The board's only recourse would have been to concede the present issue as an exception and try to prevent such circumstances from happening again, which would have been almost impossible (especially under media pressure) without an upfront stated policy.

Each school board must determine the content of its contract with enrolling families. In its admission policies and in the information given to the family, the board needs to state the conditions that would prohibit a student from enrolling or continuing to attend the school. For example, the school may decide to require the family to agree to certain religious beliefs, lifestyle practices, or family legal relationships. Some schools do invite families to enroll their children without restrictions, especially in those schools whose primary purpose is evangelism. However, schools should ask whether there are any practices that they would identify as a violation of the contract between the school and the family. Would the school continue to enroll the children under any circumstances? How would the school handle a situation in which the parents were caught selling illegal drugs at home or at school? What if the family distributed pamphlets advocating atheism or a cult? Policies—not assumptions—are needed for employees, students, and board members.

FOR REFLECTION AND DISCUSSION

1. What would you consider to be the nonnegotiables of your school?

2. What would the owner, board, administration, and parents identify as your school's nonnegotiables?

3. What are the ways in which your school currently protects and preserves these nonnegotiables?

4. What are the advantages or risks of listing these nonnegotiables in the school's covenant, rather than only stating them in board policies?

CHAPTER 8

The Covenant with the Owner

Even after defining the nonnegotiables, there still exists the challenge of determining who has authority to make changes. Other issues that need resolution include determining who is accountable to whom, the expectations for which each party is accountable, and agreement on the official process for making changes. This is an area that often brings discord in the relationship between the owner and the school board.

It is surprising how many schools do not have a clear understanding of who the owner of the school is and what role the owner plays—as distinguished from the role of the board. Perhaps this area was never raised because at the formation of the school it was obvious who the owner was and who made the decisions; the balance of authority tilted toward the owner. Perhaps the pastor of a founding church or a major donor even served as board chair. However with the passing of time and changes in the school, church, or community, the roles of the owner and school board may no longer fit into what was comfortably understood.

Under the mission-directed governance model, a written covenant between the owner and the school board is a vital tool for bringing unity. (This document is sometimes called a school constitution; in this book, *covenant* will cover both meanings.) The school covenant is a general agreement between the owner and the school board explicitly defining the responsibilities, authority, tools of control, and limits of the roles between the owner and the board.

Some schools have covenants include requirements that are irrelevant or restrictive for the best operation of the school. For example, some covenants mandate processes such as how often, where, and when the school board is to meet, what is to be on the board agenda, a list of board officers and their job descriptions, and a list of standing committees and their areas of responsibility. These operational items are superfluous to the relationship between the owner and the school board or what is necessary for good governance. Such requirements belong outside the purview of the covenant.

The covenant needs to define who the owner is, the owner's powers and limits of authority, and the process of decision making. It should clearly state that the owner empowers the school board to govern and to make policies and decisions on behalf of the owner. Substantive issues that should be included in the covenant include the major items that are of interest to the owner and the school board. (Please look at "Sample Topics to Be Included in a School Covenant with Owner," below.)

Since the school board is authorized to make policies and decisions pertaining to the school that are not prohibited or qualified in the covenant, the covenant should list any mandates or criteria that may guide or limit the board's policies, practices, and decisions. The owner will want to clearly retain authority in certain areas and will identify the means by which it will hold the board accountable. The covenant should provide a list of issues and decisions that will remain under the control of the owner.

WHO IS THE OWNER?

A school covenants identifies the owner—perhaps a church, an association of designated parents, a corporation, or even a family or an individual. However, there is often confusion regarding who is empowered to make decisions on behalf of the owner. For example, if the owner is a church, is the final decision maker the pastor or bishop, a church council, a diocese, or a majority of the church's members?

Identifying the owner raises additional questions. If the owner is an association, by what process does one become a member of the owner entity? If there are requirements for becoming a member, are they consistently enforced? If the owner is an association of parents or church members, are new members of the congregation or parents who begin to send their children to the school automatically able to vote on school matters? Is there a list of approved names of members? Are records kept of contributions made to the school by the owner, if that is a condition of membership?

Without owner definition and membership requirements, times of political confusion—if not legal battles—can arise. Picture a meeting in which the attendees are having a heated discussion over some issue; then, as the chair of the meeting with the owner is ready to call for a vote, it turns out there is debate on who may or may not vote.

DEFINING THE ROLE, AUTHORITY, AND LIMITS
OF THE OWNER AND THE BOARD

The covenant should clearly state what authority the owner will retain and the issues the owner is responsible for. For example, if the school is owned by a church or denomination, the covenant must make clear the governance role of the school board. Does the school board have merely an advisory role, with the church board or other church leaders making final decisions? If the school was founded by a church, the church leadership may see such an arrangement as a sign of strength—a way to prevent the school from departing from the basic tenets of the church. But such an arrangement has significant weaknesses. First, it eliminates the board's accountability to the church. If anything goes wrong, church leaders are responsible, even if they did not initiate the action. Second, the church is left reacting to actions taken by the board, with little opportunity to initiate action. This places church leaders in a passive role, except when they second-guess a board decision. Third, there is built-in confusion over who can make what decisions on matters such as admissions criteria, annual budget, tuition schedule, debt, or even closing the school. Fourth, this allows the church to make arbitrary and impulsive decisions without having heard firsthand the rationale for recommendations; this frequently leads to a crisis. Most people familiar with the broader Christian school movement are reminded of unfortunate examples in which owner churches decided to close their school, without benefit of open discussion with—and sometimes without the knowledge of—the school board.

Under the mission-directed governance model, the school board is authorized to govern on behalf of the owner to accomplish the mission; it also is limited by the positions and issues stated in the covenant. The covenant should clearly state that the owner is not to be involved in the board's role of governing and policymaking as long as the board is working to accomplish the mission and is operating within the stated restrictions and directives. The owner should not be allowed to vote on politically hot topics unless the school board requests it. A process could be put in place to appeal a board decision to the owner, but only if the decision is clearly in violation of the school covenant. A written policy should define the process for recalling board members and selecting new board members if the owner—whether an individual, a church, or a member association—finds the school board in violation of the school covenant.

DEFINING AND PRESERVING THE MISSION

Preserving the mission is of critical importance in light of the fact that a school must respond to changing circumstances in order to achieve its mission. The point is that the mission statement tells the school what its target is. By preserving the mission, the board affirms that the purpose of the school has been firmly established. The school leadership must not move the target. Because the mission statement articulates the purpose and direction for the school, it should be treated as a nonnegotiable and be placed under the control of the owner. Again, the primary purpose of the mission statement is to align all aspects of the school to the mandate; it is not a slogan that the school changes when launching a new promotional campaign. The vision and strategies for how to achieve the mission will change over time in response to changes in society, culture, educational expectations, and the school itself. (For example, today parents expect the ideal student to be savvy in the use of technology—something that was not the case 20 years ago.)

The school owner and community must be convinced that the board knows the target. To bring change, the board must give confidence to the school community that it can identify the nonnegotiable essentials and can discern when to stand firm and when to adapt. There will be turmoil if the school board appears to be making changes without regard for the school's philosophical foundation.

Therefore, just as the school identifies the nonnegotiables by writing them into the covenant, so it will want to place the mission statement in the covenant. The school protects these jewels by placing control of them into the hands of the owner by placing the principles in the covenant, and of the board with its policies. For example, if the mission states that the purpose of education is to cultivate discipleship in children with at least one confessing Christian parent, then the board cannot change the purpose and direction of the school to be primarily evangelistic or to be exclusively a college preparatory school without authorization by the owner.

Having the mission statement in the covenant—thus explicitly stating what the school is trying to promote and accomplish—is an important characteristic of the school that operates under the mission-directed governance model. The mission-directed governance model does allow for changes, but only of specific kinds. The school does desire to meet the changing demands of consumers, but within the context of an unchanging mission.

DEFINING ORGANIZATION AND ACCOUNTABILITY

The owner must define other requirements or limits under which the board is to operate—for example, requirements for board members, head of school, and employees—including adherence to the school's stated mission. The owner also needs to ensure that the school board will be accountable in the selection of future board members.

The covenant should require new board members to be knowledgeable in and committed to the philosophy of the school, the nonnegotiables, and the mission. The board must consider ways in which to educate and raise new potential board members who will understand and be advocates for the school's position. The new board members should enthusiastically support the obligation to protect and preserve the nonnegotiables and to advance and promote the school's philosophy and mission.

Schools governed according to the mission-directed model may enact policies and procedures that vary considerably; however, the roles of the owner and of the school board should always be clearly defined.

WHEN THE SCHOOL BOARD IS THE OWNER

There are schools and other nonprofit organizations in which the school board does own the ministry and is not accountable to anyone else. Perhaps the school has adopted a governance-by-policy model. In such cases, the concept of the covenant may still play a useful role.

When the board is the owner of the school and not accountable to another body, there are steps the board can take to preserve the mission and nonnegotiables from impulsive change. The board should clearly identify the school's founding principles.

Standard policies and board decisions normally can be approved in one meeting by a board vote that passes by a percentage as low as 51 percent. The recommended strategy to protect the founding principles is to require that these policies classified as foundational can only be changed by a board vote that is much higher—for example, requiring the change to pass by 80 to 100 percent. The process can also be slowed by requiring that the policy be approved at two successive board meetings with at least one week between the two meetings.

SAMPLE TOPICS TO BE INCLUDED IN A SCHOOL COVENANT

It is important to ensure that certain core elements are included in the covenant. Sometimes covenants will inappropriately include directions on how the board will operate, such as defining which board committees should exist and which board officers are to be elected. The following is a recommended list of items to be included in the covenant between the owner and the school board.

1. PURPOSE AND FOUNDATION OF THE SCHOOL

The covenant begins with a mission statement that identifies the purpose and ideal toward which the school should be striving. The covenant also includes references to the nonnegotiable founding principles, such as being biblically based. This first article of the covenant can include or refer to a faith statement or a theological or philosophical perspective. Both the founding nonnegotiable principles and the mission must be positioned so that they cannot be changed without the permission of the owner.

2. OWNER

This article identifies the owner and defines the owner's status. Depending on the school, the owner may be a church, a diocese, an association, or an individual. This article includes information about who is a member of the owner entity and information about owner's meetings such as formation of the agenda and voting. It then lists the responsibilities, duties, and privileges of the owner. For example, the covenant may declare that the owner is authorized to elect members of the school board, to vote to recall members of the school board, to determine whether to approve the sale or purchase of property at a specified value, and to approve covenantal changes or dissolution of the school as proposed by the school board. Having such a list of duties also means that there are limits to the owner's control. The owner may not arbitrarily interfere with the school board's governance as long as the board operates within the purposes and limits delineated in the covenant.

3. SCHOOL BOARD

The covenant clearly places into the hands of the school board the authority to govern on behalf of the owner. This article defines the number and authority of school board members and the owner's election or appointment of the board members.

This article also defines the minimum requirements to be a board member and delineates the duties of the board. For example, each board member is to be knowledgeable of and committed to protecting the nonnegotiables and is to promote the mission and foundational principles identified in the first article. This article defines term limits and the process for becoming a board member.

The covenant empowers the board to make policies and decisions about the school on behalf of the owner and to hire the head of school. This article also lists the requirements, limitations, and methods of showing accountability to the owner. The duties include authorizing and making policies regarding the school's auxiliary organizations.

4. EMPLOYEES

The covenant defines minimum requirements for school employees, such as faith position, lifestyle, church attendance, and commitment to carry out the mission of the school.

5. AMENDMENTS AND DISSOLUTION

The covenant defines the process for changing the covenant and for dissolving the school.

In summary, the covenant grants the owner control of the nonnegotiables—both the theological positions that are to be preserved and the mission statement that will keep the board's focus on what the school is to accomplish. It defines the tools of the owner's control. It authorizes the school board to govern on behalf of the owner within the covenantally established limits and purposes. The covenant clearly gives the school board the central responsibility and authority to govern the operations of the school.

FOR REFLECTION AND DISCUSSION

1. Who actually owns your school?

2. Does your school have a covenant that clearly identifies the owner?

3. In which ways is your school board accountable to the owner?

4. In your school, what would happen if the owner didn't like the school board's decision to fire a popular teacher?

5. What topics should be included in the school's covenant, and why?

CHAPTER 9

The Central Governance Authority

A covenant with the owner entrusting governance to the school board establishes agreement regarding the authority of the owner and of the school board. The board is required to carry out the school's established purposes and philosophy—both protecting the nonnegotiables and advancing the school's mission.

To ensure that the school successfully protects its nonnegotiables and strives to advance its mission, the board must establish order and predictability in the school organization. The board must develop processes and patterns of consistent decision making by ensuring that there are clear directions for operations and clear accountability. The pivotal factor is having a board that governs by policy.

Under the mission-directed governance model, the board will establish policies that define, expand, and measure the concepts articulated in the mission statement. The board writes policies by which it will govern itself. These policies include the rules the board will follow regarding such topics as board officers, board meetings and agenda, and relationships of the school board to the school head and to other employees. Policies by which the board will govern itself will be considered in subsequent chapters. Before detailing those self-governing board policies, it will be helpful to address the policies that the board directs to the school head.

HIRING THE HEAD OF SCHOOL

The board's commitment to the owner is that the goals, decisions, actions, and curriculum of the school will be in alignment with the school's philosophy and mission. To ensure that the school conforms to this pledge, the board must ensure that the school carries out these mandates. The board hires one person, the head of school, who serves as chief executive officer. This person is given the responsibility and authority for achieving the board-established goals and for operating consistently within the written board policies. The school head is directly accountable to the school board. To ensure that the head of school is accountable to the school board, it is necessary to make sure the school board or committees are not directly involved in making operational decisions.

ESTABLISHING POLICIES FOR THE SCHOOL HEAD

In order to hold the school head accountable, there must be some means to establish clear expectations, encourage corrections, or ultimately dismiss the school head when he or she is not meeting the board's standards. To make clear its expectations, the board establishes written policies authorizing the head of school to carry out the board mandates.

Policies directed to the school head are statements that identify a situation or issue on which the head of school may need to make a decision or take action. The policy identifies the standards and decision-making criteria that are germane to that concern. A board policy addressed to the school head is a directive that when confronting an identified issue, the board requires the school head to use specified criteria when making certain decisions, carrying out certain tasks, or taking certain actions. The school head may not make an exception to the written policy independently of the board; any exception must be decided by the board as a whole.

The board as a whole formally approves these written policies, and they are placed in a board policy handbook. The handbook is distributed to each board member and to the administration so that all can identify the criteria for decision making and can anticipate the expected actions. Policies have the following positive aspects:

1. They can help the organization to be well organized and managed, and can bring consistency.

2. The board, school head, and other employees can predict what the board expects.

   - The school head and others know what to do in the specified circumstances; the policies can prevent impulsive decisions in reaction to events.

   - Policies allow for the school head to take immediate action rather than wait until a committee or board meeting.

   - Policies can avoid politics because they apply regardless of who is on the board or who is an employee or donor.

3. Good policies can prevent problems and misunderstandings. By having written expectations, the school head and board do not need to guess what needs to be done and who will be responsible for implementing certain policies.

4. Good policies can protect the school head and organization from the public (media and lawsuits); and from second-guessing by an individual board member.

5. Good policies can bring accountability. The more precise the policy, the more precise is the accountability.

The school head is expected to follow all the applicable policies and practices without exception. No board member is personally involved in enforcing policies or in the daily operation of the school. The board needs to disassociate itself as much as possible from individual personalities and situations.

Having these policies avoids unstated assumptions; it also prevents the board or a committee from reviewing each incident on a case-by-case basis. If there appears to be a need to do things differently, the school head may seek the permission of the board for an exception to policy or may recommend a change in the policy. Only the board as a whole can make an exception to policy or change the board policy. Policies are not a compilation of precedents or previous board decisions. Policies are not descriptions of what was done in the past; they direct what is to be done in the future.

Promulgating a policy informs each stakeholder of the expectations, the process of assessment, and the actions that will follow if there is nonconformity. Consistent enforcement helps to create an environment that most will consider fair and equitable. Certain board and administrative policies that apply to specific audiences may be included in the family handbook or employee handbook.

The mission-directed model aims for consistency and accountability. The board governs every aspect of the school by anticipating likely situations and establishing by policy what should be done, not by making each decision separately at the time of the action. There is responsibility for the individuals, but there is also responsibility for the school community.

SAMPLE BOARD POLICIES

The following are sample policies on a variety of subjects:

School Uniforms

800. The head of school shall ensure that students wear approved uniforms at school and while under direct school supervision.

801. Uniform choices are to be determined by the head of school or designee, with selection of uniforms as arranged with one uniform company.

801.1. All uniform shirts and tops must have an embroidered school logo.

801.2. Uniforms should be compatible with school colors.

802. The head of school may make exceptions for special occasions such as "spirit days," identification of students as members of school clubs or groups, or for other reasons that enhance the school community as determined by the head of school.

Policy on Class Sizes

705. The head of school shall ensure that the numbers of students in classes are appropriate as follows:

705.1. Acceptable section sizes and appropriate projection of students to add or reduce the number of sections according to the following criteria:

Grades	Acceptable Section size	Class @ 3 sections	Class @ 4 sections	Wait list or add sections
K–2	18–22	51–67	68–88	71/93
3–4	20–24	57–75	76–96	79/101
5–6	22–26	63–83	84–108	87/113
7–12	24–28	69–87	88–116	91/121

705.2. Prekindergarten student admissions as follows or as qualified by the state social services.

Policy on Relations with Auxiliary Organizations

Auxiliary organizations are those that support the school or some specific program of the school. Examples include parent associations and booster clubs for specific school programs such as athletics and fine arts.

1401. The head of school or designee is to serve as liaison between the board and the auxiliary organizations.

1402. The head of school is to guide the auxiliary organizations to follow the board policies including the following:

1402.1. Ensure that the board recognizes the auxiliary organizations as being part of _____ Christian School.

1402.2. Ensure that the board approves the covenant agreement and proposed changes of the auxiliary organization between it and the school board.

1402.3. Approve or seek approval by the school board of the auxiliary organization's budget, designated expenditures, fundraising activities over $2,000, purchases requiring city permits, or purchases that appears to restrict the long-range plan of the school.

SCHOOL HEAD ADMINISTRATIVE POLICIES

Whether a policy is a board policy or an administrative policy does make a difference. The policy's status determines who wrote the policy and consequently who is authorized to change the policy or make an exception to it. Since board policies are passed by the school board, only the school board can make a change or exception; the school head is not empowered to make or alter a board policy. The school head writes administrative policies and is authorized to change them if needed as long as they are in compliance with board policies. Teachers or other employees may not change administrative policies.

The board generally gives the head of school as much leeway as possible in the methods of carrying out the board policies. The intent is to allow the school head to be resourceful and creative in order to successfully lead the school toward accomplishing its mission. Once policies and goals are set, the head of school can be more flexible and free to work without direct board interference, as long as the methods are not contrary to board policies.

The head of school cannot personally enforce each policy, so the head delegates certain matters to principals or other designated persons. To increase employee accountability, the head of school articulates expectations by writing administrative policies or procedures to guide employees in their decision making. The administration, rather than the board, may thus determine some policies—or at least their details and implementation.

For example, the board will have policies directed to the school head that regulate school finances. The school head will write administrative policies and procedures that regulate (for example) who may make purchases for the school, who may use the school credit card and under what circumstances, and how money will be regulated, collected, deposited, and distributed.

For another example, the school board will have health and safety policies. The school head will write administrative policies that guide the custodians, bus drivers, and those who prepare and serve meals. Many of the administrative policies are the details of requirements and processes that are the substance of staff and student handbooks. Other administrative policies will address issues such as employee dress code, attendance, and use of school computers.

One final illustration is evaluation of teachers. Under the mission-directed model, the board governs by a policy that requires the head of school to evaluate teachers. The administrator will establish more detailed administrative policies that list the specific criteria to be used, the circumstances under which and how often observations are to be conducted, and what is to be done with the results. These policies would be included in the faculty handbook.

IDENTIFYING BOARD-ONLY DECISIONS

The board establishes policies that give mandates and decision-making limits to the school head. However, there are areas in which the board delegates to the school head the authority to initiate or recommend a course of action, but the board requires that it make the final decision. Board policies should identify these issues. The following are examples of issues that the school head should bring before the board for a final conclusion:

- *Approving the annual budget.* One of the most effective ways the board controls the direction and priorities of the school is through the annual budget. If the budget includes an administrative request for an expanded curriculum, additional teachers, facility improvements, etc., the board will need to authorize those expenditures.

- *Approving capital projects.* The board needs to approve projects requiring fund-raising and development outside of the budget, such as buildings, land, or purchase of new technology equipment.

- *Approving the purchase or sale of property or other major assets.*

- *Approving recommendations that will be presented to the owner for changes in the school covenant and bylaws.*

- *Approving new policies or amendments to current board policies.*

- *Approving the recommendation of board candidates to the owner.*

- *Approving exceptions to board policy.* The head of school is responsible for ensuring that all decisions consistently follow the board policies. If the head of school thinks there may be a case that merits an exception, the head must present the case to the full board. Since the board as a whole determines policy, the board as a whole (not just one board member or a committee) is required to grant any exceptions. The board as a whole maintains authority and control. The board should be aware that granting exceptions to policies may set a precedent and likely will require the policy to be rewritten.

- *Hearing and judging appeals to administrative decisions.* If a person such as a parent or employee thinks he or she has been dealt with unjustly, the person can appeal to the school board for a ruling.

- *Determining school direction and priorities.* The board provides a mandate for the head of school on how the energy and resources of the school should be focused.

- *Determining which reports the head of school is required to submit regarding information on and evaluation of various school programs.*

- *Holding the head of school accountable.* The board hires the head of school, evaluates the head of school's job performance, and awards the head of school's annual employment contract and conditions. Only the school board can determine the salary and benefits of the school head.

All board members should have a written board policy handbook that states these policies and principles of operation. The handbook should be brought up-to-date as the board adds, deletes, or amends its policies.

Under the mission-directed governance model the role of the school board is to govern and direct the school. The head of school manages and runs the school with accountability to the board. Every aspect of the school is accountable to the school board.

FOR REFLECTION AND DISCUSSION

1. Why is it important that the board hire the head of school?

2. How do board policies hold the head of school accountable to the board?

3. How do board policies give freedom to the head of school to accomplish the board's mandates?

4. Why should the board operate by policies instead of making individual decisions as issues arise?

5. What is the difference between a board policy and an administrative policy?

CHAPTER 10

The Process of Writing Board Policies

Writing policies for the first time can be an intimidating task. How can board members anticipate what should be a policy, and how a policy should be written? Do board members need to write policies to cover every contingncy? The process is more manageable than one would think, and it can be broken down into steps.

IDENTIFYING TOPICS THAT MERIT BEING WRITTEN AS POLICY

A workable process for considering policies begins with the formation of several ad hoc committees composed of a few board members and the head of school. Depending on the topic, the board could consider having one or two other administrators or other employees participate as well.

The purpose of these ad hoc committees is to discern what present school practices and expectations might be considered for potential policies. If the school is moving from a traditional governance model, the easiest way to determine appropriate manageable topics is to assign each ad hoc committee a topic that had been normally considered by a standing committee under the traditional governance model. The ad hoc committee will identify the responsibilities, issues, and practices the standing committee had considered year after year, and then determine how these issues would be recognized, how the issues should normally be resolved, and what criteria were assumed. The following may stimulate thinking of examples of issues commonly considered by standing committees that would merit formation as a policy:

- *Admissions.* Admissions policies would likely include minimum student academic ability, behavior standards, tuition payment, health issues, and parent or guardian custodial issues. The board may have requirements as to parents' or students' religious position or church attendance, or at least the requirement to sign an acknowledgment and acceptance of what the school will teach.

- *Finances.* The board needs policies for bookkeeping standards and reports, tuition assistance, banking, collection and disbursement of funds, and the budget process. The board may establish policies requiring an outside accounting firm to perform periodic financial reviews or audits as well as policies regarding financial records, insurance, investments, and tuition schedule.

- *Education.* The board will establish policies that address class size, accreditation, and curriculum.

- *Facilities.* Board policies will include a requirement to meet standards for health and safety, insurance, and transportation.

- *Promotion and development.* The board will want to approve major projects for which money can be raised, as well as set certain limits for the process of fund-raising.

- *Student services and expectations.* The board will establish general policies regarding attendance, student discipline, and dress; policies that guide student social activities, counseling, and chapel offerings; policies that govern extracurricular offerings such as athletics and student clubs and organizations; and policies regarding expectations for out-of-school behavior.

- *Personnel.* The board will likely establish policies regarding employment, salary and benefits packages, and employee evaluation. The board may also set qualifications and conditions for employment such as requiring the employees to be Christians, to be certified (for teachers), and to send the employees' eligible children to the school. Policies should cover topics such as hiring and the reasons the school head may not hire some candidates. Additional policies may include directions for termination, employee classification, employee evaluation, and an employee grievance procedure.

- *Auxiliary organizations.* These organizations can be very beneficial and provide support and funding for programs that otherwise would significantly add to tuition. Examples include parent associations, foundations for endowments, school-owned for-profit businesses, and specialty organizations that support specific programs such as athletics, fine arts, alumni, special education, and special travel experiences. The board should establish policies that require the board to officially recognize the existence of all auxiliary organizations. The board should require each auxiliary organization to establish a covenant with and be formally approved by the board, and board approval should be required for any proposed changes to the covenant by the organization.

The board also needs to establish the means of controlling the efforts and direction and priorities of the auxiliary organizations so that they support the broader school priorities. For example, the school may establish a policy requiring the auxiliary organization to secure permission from the school board before launching plans for major purchases or campaigns.

- *Other topics that merit policy consideration:* volunteers; counseling; promotion; and relationships with home, church, and government. The board may also require the school head to submit a strategic plan.

Under the mission-directed governance model, the board also writes policies related to the school's philosophy, mission, nonnegotiables, and means of measurement.

DISTINGUISHING BOARD POLICIES FROM ADMINISTRATIVE POLICIES

The board identifies the policies that the board wants to be in its domain and what policies the board permits the administrator to be free to write and change. It is important to remember that a board policy is a statement, position, or requirement that only the board as a whole can change. The school head may change administrative policies only.

POLICY FORMAT

Policies usually are layered as to the amount of detail they cover. Board policies directed to the school head typically declare in the first statement that the head of school is accountable for the specified topical category. The process is similar to writing an outline for a theme paper with major headings and subheadings.

The board may write policies as general or as specific as it feels comfortable. For example, the board may write a board policy requiring the school head to write policies regarding student health. It is then up to the school head to write administrative policies regarding issues such as handling of student medication. On the other hand, the board may deem it wise to write certain policies regarding student behavior to be board policies, for examples, policies dealing with major cultural challenges, such as shifts from traditional moral standards regarding human sexuality.

Whatever is not specified by board policy is left to the discretion of the head of school. For example, the board may establish a policy on student uniforms, delegating to the school head the enforcement of student dress codes. The board policy could be quite specific and detailed, or the board policy could be more general, stating that students are to wear school-approved uniforms, leaving to the school head to determine in administrative policies what the uniforms are to look like.

The board may want to write some policies to be very specific and detailed. For example the board would likely want to write the policy setting the faculty salary schedule as this would ensure that the school head cannot negotiate a separate salary with an individual teacher.

There is no formula to determine the level of detail. Some policy categories may be quite short. For example, the board may require the school head to develop appropriate administrative policies regarding safety and health issues that ensure the school's compliance with federal, state, and local laws and regulations in areas such as these:

- State-mandated child abuse policy
- Pesticides policy
- OSHA-mandated policies on bloodborne pathogens
- Accident policy
- Medicine policy

For other issues, the board may define the limits of the school head in more detail rather than leaving such policies to the discretion of the administrator. Examples of policies that may contain more detailed elements include employee contracts, admissions, and finance.

WRITING POLICIES POSITIVELY

There are some who advocate that board policies be written in the negative to emphasize that the CEO has authority over any actions that do not overstep the limitations listed. So instead of saying "the executive director should …" they recommend the policy be written as "the school head may not …" or "the school head shall not fail to …." The purpose is largely symbolic, emphasizing that the executive director must work within the limits but is free to use any method or program not limited by policies.

The mission-directed governance model does not suggest that policies be written in the negative. Too many people are confused by the negative, especially when a policy is written using double negatives (e.g., "the school head shall not fail not to…"). Rather than symbolically defining the limits of the CEO's authority, it is better to write a policy in such a way that everyone immediately understands the purposes and the limitations of the policy.

Another reason the mission-directed governance model recommends stating policies positively is to encourage the board to create policies that give general mandates to the school head for advancing the school's mission in a certain an area or to state the goal that the board wants the head to strive for. For example, for personnel, the board may decide to create the following policy with its subareas:

600. The school head shall make every effort to employ mature Christians qualified to accomplish their areas of responsibility. Accordingly, the school head shall ensure that employees meet the following qualifications and conditions of employment....

The school board may want to introduce its expectations regarding student discipline with a policy such as the following:

801. The school seeks to promote values and behaviors that are consistent with those representing the kingdom of Christ. _____ Christian School has an obligation both to the individual student and to the school community. The school is interested in both preventing problems as well as helping people deal with problems. Therefore, the school head shall establish administrative policies and student behavior expectations that promote an orderly school organization and encourage student conduct that supports Christian relationships and enhances the school's philosophy and goals. Therefore the school head shall....

DOES THE SCHOOL REALLY NEED ALL THOSE POLICIES?

Some people advocate that the CEO should have as much latitude as possible, and that therefore the organization should have minimal policies directed to the CEO except to require actions that are legal, prudent, and, ethical.

Under the mission-directed governance model the board is encouraged to make policies for most categories germane to the school, such as education, finances, and admissions. The reason for such board policies is to prevent misunderstanding and to protect the school head. The board will want to give final authorization for each organizational area even if the school head proceeds with the best motives and is both prudent and ethical. It is not that any of the motives or the actions are bad; it simply is best if the board approves these actions by policy and does not merely allow the school head to take these actions to achieve the results.

In a Christian school setting, it is particularly important to establish board policies for the school head in the various categories of school administration. The authority of the school head as CEO is very powerful. The school needs board policies to guide the school head in the right direction and to have policies that act as protective fences around potentially dangerous areas of school leadership.

Here are a few examples of actions taken by various school heads; in each case, the school head acted with good intentions. One can imagine how these actions could be very hazardous and very controversial if they were activated without board authorization.

- Intended result: improve schoolwide academic test scores. Planned action: change admissions standards so that only students who can prove their academic superiority may enroll.

- Intended result: have students spend more time in the classroom to improve academic test scores. Planned action: change the school calendar so that the school meets year-round, and increase the length of the school day.

- Intended result: Improve the school image in athletics. Planned action: hire a prestigious athletic director or head coach who has played on professional sports teams, who is a very gregarious moral person, but who is not a Christian.

- Intended result: encourage teachers to strive for high academic performance. Planned action: launch a merit pay incentive by giving some good teachers a bonus or a higher salary than other teachers.

ORGANIZING AND IDENTIFYING POLICIES

In order to organize the policies to be able to find them when they are needed, the board should identify each topical category as a separate section numbered in sequence. For example, in the sample board policy handbook in appendix A of this book, section 100 includes the school's covenant with the owner, state and federal acknowledgement that the school is a tax-exempt organization, and other charter documents. Section 200 contains the school's motto, mission, philosophy, goals, core curricular principles, and standards of measurement. Section 300 lists the policies that pertain to governance, including the identity of the owner (individual or group); policies by which the board governs itself, such as purpose, expectations of relationships among board members, officers and tasks; and board committees along with their purposes and limitations. Section 400 lists policies that define the board's relationship with employees.

Each detailed subordinate policy is placed under the appropriate section heading and given an extended number following a sequential outline format. As more detailed policies are identified, each is given a number. Using section 200 as an example, the school's motto is 201, mission statement 202, statement of philosophy 203, school goals 204, and so forth. A policy that is a subset of a primary topic is given a more detailed number: for example, under section 204 (School Goals), the board may decide to list specific school goals, identified as 204.1, 204.2, 204.3, and so on.

BOARD POLICY HANDBOOK

The board policy handbook is a compilation of all the policies the board has approved; it is distributed as one document or folder to all board members and administrators. The board policy handbook gives all board members and administrators the same goals, rules of procedure, and criteria for reporting and accountability. Making sure in a formal way that all have the same information prevents mistaken assumptions, inconsistent recall of previous board minutes, and speculation. If it is necessary to change a policy, the board can make the change. As long as the change does not involve a topic that must be submitted to the owner, the board can modify the policy with precise wording to accomplish the purpose.

It may be helpful to make a current board policy handbook available to faculty and staff. It is difficult to continuously keep current many board policy handbooks, and the faculty and staff do not typically have the need to frequently refer to board policies, so for the purpose of being transparent and keeping employees informed, it may be helpful to place a hard copy of the most recently updated board policy handbook in the staff lounge, workroom, or office, or post the most current digital copy on a server that is accessible to faculty and staff.

AD HOC COMMITTEE REPORTS TO THE BOARD

The ad hoc committees preparing potential board policies will periodically make presentations to the board for discussion and to determine whether the conclusions are accurate and accepted by the board—along with noted corrections or additions. Eventually, conclusions approved by the board may be used to update the board policy manual.

The board will approve the draft of accepted policies. These policies are usually not implemented immediately, but the draft policies will allow the ad hoc committees to begin the process of determining policies in other sections until all the section categories are written in the form of policies. The board then reviews each category one more time. When an ad hoc committee completes its objectives, the committee is disbanded.

It is recommended that at the end of this process of identifying school areas, writing policies, and review by the school board, the board will have discussion and prayer on the recommended policies. The question at the end of the process is for the board to decide whether to adopt these policies in accordance with the mission-directed governance model.

FOR REFLECTION AND DISCUSSION

1. Why is it helpful to have board policies that govern employee contracts, admissions, and auxiliary organizations?

2. What are the risks if the board does not operate by written policies?

3. What are some specific areas in which your school operates by written policies?

4. If your school has recently written new policies or modified existing policies, describe and evaluate the process that was used.

CHAPTER 11

The Role of the Head of School

The Christian school exists to influence the lives of students and to guide them in their thinking, behavior, and service to Christ's kingdom, both now and in the future. The board accepts the responsibility of ensuring that the school's mission will be advanced. Student learning, and therefore the relationships that promote growth in discipleship and application, must be the primary focus of the school. The *head of school* is accountable to the board for every aspect of the school to ensure that student learning is the most effective it can be. (Some schools might use another title such as *superintendent, headmaster, principal,* or *administrator.*) So what kind of person should the board seek as head of school?

The head of school is expected to be visionary, proactive, and able to accomplish the directives established by the board in a way that advances the school's mission and philosophy. Since the head of school plays a central role, the board must consider candidates carefully, and then provide continual encouragement and advice after the position is filled. Rather than reducing the head of school's responsibilities to a job description that states the usual involvement in finance, promotion, curriculum, and the like, it may be helpful to consider the general nature of this leadership position.

It is assumed that the board requires candidates to have the necessary personal Christian commitment, character and integrity, academic training and credentials, love for children and young people, and the qualifications and experience to serve in this capacity. The head of school must personally model Christian living, piety, and scholarship.

The board should be looking for a candidate who will accomplish the mission. Jim Collins, author of *Good to Great,* points out that the best CEOs are not the stereotypical charismatic, flamboyant, high-profile leaders; the best leaders exhibit modesty, humility, and tenacity to accomplish the mission (2001, 30).

> It is very important to grasp that Level 5 leadership is not just about humility and modesty. It is equally about ferocious resolve, an almost stoic determination to do whatever needs to be done to make the company great.

The mission-directed model requires that the head of school be a leader rather than have only management skills. First, the head of school needs an understanding of and commitment to the school's philosophy and mission. Second, the head of school must have a passion to accomplish the mission and a vision of how to make progress toward the mission. Third, the head of school needs to understand education theory and pedagogy to support student learning and teaching. Fourth, the head of school must work well with people to accomplish common goals. Fifth, the head of school must be a good administrator, with organization and management skills.

These characteristics make the difference between wishing for whole-life discipleship for students and initiating processes to actually make things happen. The head of school must be able to assess the school's present circumstances and determine appropriate steps and priorities in light of the school's needs, circumstances, and resources in order to lead the school toward accomplishing the mission.

PHILOSOPHY AND MISSION

The head of school leads the school in holding and advancing the vision, philosophy, and mission around which the school unites. The head of school is the first line of defense of the nonnegotiables and the first in line to concretely advance the philosophy and mission. The school community must have confidence that this leader can initiate proposals that advance the mission but also is a person who has a solid foundation in, comprehensive understanding of, and firm commitment to the foundational beliefs.

Heads of school must be able to present, explain, and teach the school's philosophy to all members of the school community to ensure that educational curriculum, programs, and school operations maintain integrity with the school's philosophy and mission.

VISION AND ENTREPRENEURSHIP

The head of school must have a passion for the students and for the calling to nurture them to become whole-life disciples. He or she must inspire others to creatively imagine new possibilities that will help identify and pursue this ideal. This calls for vision and the ability to uncover needs and discern new opportunities to improve student learning. The head of school helps the school community form and translate its vision and mission into practical application throughout the fabric and culture of the school.

The head of school creates a climate for developing new ideas and vision for the school. Vision and ideas can come from any part of the school constituency, including parents and students, but arise especially from teachers and administrators. The head of school must inspire others to be willing to make changes necessary for constant improvement, and will normally be the initiator of or advocate for visionary proposals and projects. A vision is more than a collection of individual creative ideas. The visionary leader should be able to combine and coordinate ideas so that they effectively contribute to the mission.

The board typically does not generate vision by suggesting initiatives and programs, but it is still responsible for the school's vision. The board's role is to understand the role of vision and to assess thoughts and proposals by considering them in light of the mission, budget, and other school priorities. In order to support and guide visionary thinking, the board allocates money, time, and people, and establishes standards of measurement. Board members need not feel guilty that they do not originate ideas for change; this is not their usual responsibility. Of course, it is good if board members do suggest new ideas, but they usually are not in a position to do so. The board typically is not composed of trained educators, and even if some are, serving on the board is an avocation. Moreover, the board does not have the daily contact with staff necessary to assess needs or establish procedures for implementation. Board members' ideas and proposals generally are given to the head of school, who then reports back to the board on feasibility, cost, and so on.

The head of school is trained in educational theory, is familiar with its application, and can anticipate implications for the organizational structure. The head of school is the educational and organizational leader. If the school makes the mistake of hiring a mere manager, the school may be well managed, but it will have a difficult time advancing the mission. Without vision, the school—board members, faculty, administrators, and constituency—will lose its mission focus and revert back to identifying and solving problems.

Boards can cultivate vision in administrators by supporting professional development, sending them to conferences, encouraging formal course work in continuing education, and ensuring that they are networked with like-minded administrators from other institutions. Boards may require a report from heads of school on their own professional development, what they have learned, and what they are likely to implement.

EDUCATION AND PEDAGOGY

The central activity and purpose of operating a school is to influence student learning. The head of school must understand education, how students learn, and the implications for the teaching process. This means that the head of school needs a clear understanding and vision of curriculum, discipleship, and student learning. The chief executive officer must have unconditional passion for the school's philosophy and vision, as well as love for and knowledge of students, teachers, and the complexities of the educational experience.

Schools may underestimate the need for educational vision and leadership by offering the administrator position to a teacher who has performed some service requiring management skills such as scheduling athletic contests, planning transportation routes, or preparing the course schedule. These skills are helpful, but they should not be the defining element when looking for a visionary educational leader.

Though heads of school should be familiar with educational issues primarily, it is unfortunate that so many excellent educators who become administrators are not adequately trained in business management. The head of school needs training in finance, fund-raising, promotion, organization, running a meeting, and strategic planning.

TEAM BUILDING

Success is not achieved because of the work of one individual; it comes as the result of many people working together in a common cause. The head of school must work well with diverse people; provide communication, participation, and delegation; and bring consensus, cooperation, and movement toward common goals. He or she must provide leadership toward the ideal, working with board, staff, students, and community.

The school head will find it necessary to have an administrative team or at least a few key teachers to consult with in order to assess what can be done and how quickly. These key team members are usually those who will be influential in communicating with other faculty so that all the staff understand and are motivated to accomplish the goals.

The head of school needs a passion to encourage, develop, prepare, and support teachers and staff by providing clear expectations and resource support. Working closely for and with the school board, the head of school must make every effort to be personally and professionally accountable to and a servant of the board, as the board ultimately is responsible for the ministry. This requires communicating with integrity, bringing full disclosure, and consistently insisting that all participants adhere to policies.

The head of school must recognize people's strengths and weaknesses as they contribute to the ministry. He or she must be open and compassionate to individual personal circumstances, acting as an advocate for people and an encourager of the administrative team, faculty, and staff.

To form consensus, the head of school must be visible and available to students, staff, parents, board members, those who serve in auxiliary organizations, volunteers, major donors, pastors, and the general Christian school community. The head of school must promote and articulate Christian education not only to school constituents but also to the broader community.

It is important and valuable for the head of school to spend time with people, not only in meetings but also listening to and resolving concerns. The head of school needs a reputation for listening to people and carefully evaluating observations, complaints, and ideas. But the head of school also must be one who can say yes and no as necessary. This can prevent problems rather than merely correcting already existing ones. It also permits the administrator to see the whole picture and maintain a balance of priorities.

ORGANIZATION AND MANAGEMENT

The head of school must be an effective manager; this includes being organized, efficient, and practical. The head of school is expected to have basic management skills such as time management, establishing deadlines, and making meetings worthwhile and productive.

Good organizational skills help translate the mission and vision into the fabric of the school—melding vision, educational process, people, and organization. This requires broad previous experience, perhaps in other roles, in order to be able to recognize what works and how to avoid common pitfalls. Heads of school must generate the structure, accountability, and encouragement that lead to success in reaching the goals.

The school head should be more like an entrepreneur than merely a manager. Too often the manager is only concerned about efficiently maintaining the status quo. While good maintenance is important, the school is more likely to prosper if the school head is an entrepreneur who spurs board and staff toward innovative and creative ways to advance the mission.

Managerial and entrepreneurial leadership should include brainstorming, initiating, identifying, and encouraging change and new ideas. When guiding ideas, programs, and projects—whether introduced by staff, parents, or students—the head of school must see to it that all people and groups follow procedures to accomplish their goal by advising on processes and communicating likely responses.

The head of school needs a sense of strategic planning with the ability to understand and evaluate the history and context of the school's needs and circumstances. This role requires helping the board to anticipate opportunities, challenges, and risks; it includes making special reports and giving guidance in policy formation and review. Since board membership changes, the head of school brings continuity from year to year at the primary leadership level. This provides the experience and history that a board needs as it analyzes programs, policies, and the future of the school.

The head of school should understand the mission-directed model of governance and organization, including policies, reports and accountability, and the process for reaching the vision. The head of school promotes accountability by establishing clear goals, criteria for measurement, and timelines. This also includes shepherding—following up and reminding people of responsibilities and deadlines so that assignments are completed. There is a natural decline in momentum in accomplishing scheduled tasks. New, urgent items appear on everyone's agenda. Memories fade as to who was supposed to do what.

The position of head of school also requires scheduling around deadlines, getting items on agendas, and encouraging staff and others to deal with their commitments in a timely way. The head of school must anticipate what is coming and should be aware of and work on issues that may be months or years in the future. This means frequently planning for contingencies that may never occur and preparing for a variety of approaches to coming situations. The head of school needs a clear understanding of what resources are needed, are available, or can be developed.

Under the mission-directed governance model, the board controls the direction and priorities of the school, and the head of school is responsible for seeing that the mission, philosophy, and vision are implemented.

RESPONSIBILITIES OF THE SCHOOL HEAD

The mission-directed governance model may change the head of school's role and expectations. One question that arises with so much on the head of school's task list is whether responsibility for all these projects will cause increased pressure and require more time or additional personnel. Since there are so many other evening obligations (concerts, plays, programs, athletic events, and so on) this requires an unusual sacrifice from the head of school's family.

The mission-directed model will not reduce the number of concerts and events at which the head of school must appear; however, the head of school's time may be a bit more manageable. Under the mission-directed governance model the head of school is more likely to meet with people during regular working hours rather than at evening meetings. It is easier to schedule meetings for breakfast or during the day with such people as the director of transportation, director of curriculum, director of facilities, and admissions director; it is easier to meet with the principals and other members of an administrative team. The mission-directed governance model also allows the head of school to be more efficient, with a clearer idea of what the priorities are. Spending time on vision is much more enjoyable than addressing only problems. The educational leader is more motivated to spend time on these issues. Making a difference in the lives of students was likely the primary reason the head of school entered the profession in the first place.

Probably the greatest stress reliever is that the head of school has the joy of knowing what he or she is responsible to accomplish. Political issues are minimized because the board has previously determined the leadership projects and priorities.

FOR REFLECTION AND DISCUSSION

1. Do you think the head of school should have a background as an educator? Why or why not?

2. Why is it essential that the head of school be the primary person tasked to further the school's vision?

3. Why should the head of school be more like an entrepreneur than a manager?

4. What can a school do to stimulate and encourage the head of school to develop more of an attitude of entrepreneurship?

CHAPTER 12

How the Board Governs Itself

The board is accountable to the owner for protecting the nonnegotiables and advancing the mission of the school. The school board must act as a unified body that gives guidance and direction to the school, holding the head of school accountable for carrying out board mandates.

Acting as a unified body is tough and does not happen naturally. What can the board do to draw people and ideas together? This is deeper than having social times together, although that is a sensible and enjoyable practice. When business must get done, how does the board cultivate respect and trust between board members, the head of school, and others involved in its discussions and actions?

It is important to have a congenial professional atmosphere, mutual trust, and respect in board meetings. The experience of serving on a board should be satisfying, and each member should feel fortunate to be serving with such wise people. Each participant is to humbly recognize that the group is achieving something greater than any one person could accomplish. Two things will help develop this atmosphere: first, emphasizing common ground rather than adversarial expectations; second, conducting business in a predictable, orderly, and meaningful manner.

Board meetings should provide an environment that encourages lively discussion, a diversity of opinions, and many options for addressing important questions. The board should be confident that the discussion is based on relevant information that will help it toward unified conclusions and actions. To cultivate this sense of common direction and predictability of process, the board must establish policies that define its own operations and procedures to ensure that it is carrying out the mandate established by the owner.

BOARD POLICIES THAT LIMIT THE ROLE OF INDIVIDUAL BOARD MEMBERS

Policies on board operations are necessary for the board to limit its own actions and stay focused on the primary issues. For example, there needs to be agreement on the conditions and processes to call an individual board member out of order. Board members must know the extent and limits of their own role and authority, when they are authorized to speak as a board member, and when is it out of order for them to make decisions and take personal action.

Under the mission-directed governance model, only the board as a whole has authority. No individual board member may speak or act on behalf of the board or make independent decisions or interpretations unless granted permission by a board policy or by a specific decision of the whole board for a particular action. When not participating in direct board responsibilities, an individual board member is a parent, volunteer, major donor, or other constituent. When serving as a volunteer, for instance, the board member is under the authority of the school-designated supervisor.

Suggested board policies regarding board operations include the following:

- The board always operates as board-as-a-whole, with no authority resting with individual board members.

- While the use and limits of committees will be raised in a couple of chapters, it is worth stating here that the board should have very few standing committees. These committees must have purposes and limits—defined by policy—for ensuring that the school head is on task and conforming to policies. Committees are not for decision making.

- The board establishes policies stating the minimum qualifications and requirements that board members must have in order to serve.

- The board establishes policies regarding the relationship between the board and the school head.

- The board establishes policies defining relationships between the board the staff.

- The board establishes policies as to how board members get something added to the board agenda.

Because an individual board member's authority is limited to participation in board meetings, or as otherwise determined by the whole board, the role the individual board member may play when communicating to a member of the constituency or an employee is also limited. To maintain the correct lines of authority, the board member should not wander into the responsibilities of the head of school. Such communication limitations will maintain correct lines of authority, allow the governance model to bring resolution and reconciliation, and provide consistent communication.

It also is important that each board member act responsibly as a trustee, focusing on what is in the best interests of the school as a whole. Board members are not to represent a certain group of constituents (e.g., parents, church members, or auxiliary organizations) or to advance particular causes at the expense of what may be best for the school.

BOARD COMMUNICATION WITH CONSTITUENCY AND SCHOOL EMPLOYEES

Another reason for limiting an individual board member's communication is to promote resolution of conflicts and bring reconciliation. Some constituents or employees think board members can cut through red tape and resolve a conflict. If parents want action to change a grade, get their child more playing time on the team, or ameliorate a disciplinary consequence, the board member is not in a position to correct the problem. If an employee complains about a work duty, poor allocation of resources, or pay, the board member does not have authority to personally resolve the problem.

The board member must not get too personally involved, because if an issue is not resolved at the administrative level, it may eventually come to the board on appeal, and the board member must not be in a conflict of interest by having already indicated a position on the issue. Instead, the board member should listen and then advise where the constituent or employee can go to get the problem addressed. For most problems, the most assertive the board member should be is to contact the teacher, coach, or head of school and ask that person to deal directly with the issue and seek resolution.

It is important to remember that the lines of communication should follow the biblical principles outlined in Matthew 18.

> If your brother or sister sins, go and point out their fault, just between the two of you. If they listen to you, you have won them over. But if they will not listen, take one or two others along, so that "every matter may be established by the testimony of two or three witnesses." If they still refuse to listen, tell it to the church; and if they refuse to listen even to the church, treat them as you would a pagan or a tax collector. (Matthew 18:15–17)

When dealing with a problem, one should keep the emotion and rhetoric as private and low-key as possible. A parent who has a disagreement with a teacher must address it with the teacher first. If there is no resolution, then the school head may be involved. If there is still no resolution, then the parent may appeal to the school board. The principles of Matthew 18 work! They were given to help resolve issues.

Most problems can be resolved if they are approached in a gentle manner that allows an explanation or a reconsideration of an action. Public arguments, rallying of allies, and threats of power usually do not bring reconciliation, but rather a win/lose mentality.

The board member must guard the integrity of the board and encourage those with complaints to follow the principles of Matthew 18:

- If the employee or constituent decides to complain, the board member should listen only to enough of the detail to point the complainant to the right person in the Matthew 18 sequence. If the complainant is reluctant to follow Matthew 18, the board member may ask the other party, principal, or head of school to contact the complainant to attempt to get the issue resolved. The board member should not try to personally resolve or even indicate support of the complaint. The school should have a policy that spells out a grievance procedure.

- If the case does eventually come before the board on appeal, the board member should have retained his or her integrity so that he or she can be objective. A board member who publicly supports a position does not bring resolution but rather politicizes and polarizes the issues into win/lose antagonisms.

- If the constituent or employee has a good idea for improvement, the board member should likewise refer the person to the head of school or to the appropriate person responsible for that area.

An exception to this may come if the complaint is serious, such as actions that are illegal, dangerous, or immoral. There may be circumstances in which the issue is larger than a personal offense; in such cases an employee or parent should contact a supervisor who can address the issue.

Limiting the individual board member's role aids consistent communication. If the head of school is to actually serve as chief executive officer of the school and be accountable to the school board, the board must ensure that the head of school is given full authority to carry out the role, including being the main spokesperson for the school. The head of school will speak to the constituency and employees on behalf of the school and announce resolutions, even board conclusions (unless the resolution is about the head of school). This allows everyone to get the same information at the same time. If individual board members independently announce a board decision, the result is a gossip trail in which people speculate about who knows what and what accounts are reliable.

When should there be direct communication between a school board member and employees and constituency? The board member should publicly support the decisions of the school and give information on the philosophy of the school, its importance, and the progress being made. The board members should encourage support from the employees and parents. Board members have a required role in promoting, advancing, and advertising the school. No employee or member of the constituency is expected to exhibit more support than the board does. If the board members are not enthusiastic about the school, why should anyone else be? The board must be the most convinced and articulate on the necessity of Christian education in general and the specific mission of this particular school. A key role of the board member is to help explain and "sell" the rationale for new ideas. For example, a board member should be able to explain the rationale for a new building program, an increase in tuition, or a new governance model, and the good board member will support the school with conversations about the wonderful things going on, the outstanding teachers, and the effective programs.

Board members are networked with businesses, churches, and members of the community; therefore, board members have credibility and access to key constituencies that no one else has. Board members often know of possible partnerships and potential resources that school employees have no way of discovering. Board members are crucial in personal giving and in working with the development director to introduce acquaintances to ministry support opportunities.

To maintain their integrity, board members may use the following guidelines for appropriate communications:

- Give the story of the positive things going on at the school.

- Give the results of board actions (issues already considered and publicly concluded).

- If the social circumstances require further conversation, support the conclusion with some of the rationale and explain why this action was thought to be in the best interest of the school.

There are rare times when the board speaks directly to the constituency or employees without the head of school, but these usually are covered by policies or board actions. The board should meet before any statements are made public in order to determine what the board's position is and whether one or more board members will be allowed to speak for the board. Such exceptions include the following:

- If an action or personal life concern of the head of school is the issue (e.g., if the board just hired or fired the head of school)

- If the board is reporting to the owner

- If the board is soliciting observations as part of evaluating the head of school

- If the board calls upon members to participate in gaining information for the school, e.g., in town hall meetings (In these cases it is important to remember that the purpose of the board contacts with constituents and employees is to find trends, not to solve individual complaints. On this basis the board will determine direction and priorities. Such occasions usually are conducted in partnership with the head of school.)

- If individual board members work with the development director or head of school to solicit funds

- If the board sees a need to meet with the constituency in order to explain board positions, vision, or actions (This should be done by a board member only when the board as a whole decides that this option is better than having the head of school explain the matter.)

BOARD MEETINGS AND AGENDA

The board needs policies that delineate how the board agenda is determined. The agenda and priorities should be formed by consensus of the whole board, not subject to the whim of an individual board member.

The mission-directed model recommends that board policy specify one or two board meetings per year that provide an opportunity for board members to brainstorm and suggest school programs for evaluation or topics the board should consider at future meetings. These suggested topics are given to the board's executive committee, which considers them in consultation with the head of school and places them on a board calendar. Topics are assigned to the agenda for specific board meetings throughout the year. The list is presented to the board, which may make suggestions for changes; in the end the full board must approve the listing of topics and dates. Board members and the administration will then know which issues will be raised at which board meetings, allowing everyone to come prepared. This ensures agreed-upon priority being given to important issues and prevents introduction of personal issues. True emergency issues can be introduced to the board by the board president.

SAMPLE BOARD AGENDA POLICY

302.4.7. The annual agenda will include opportunities for board members to submit suggestions for items to be included on the annual board agenda.

302.4.7.1. The executive committee is to consider board member suggestions for the board agenda and to prepare a tentative agenda for the following year's meetings. The chair will determine the agenda for any particular meeting, including emergency issues.

302.4.7.2. Any board member desiring to recommend any additional matter for board discussion will advise the chair of such a matter at least ten (10) days prior to the scheduled board meeting.

ROLE OF THE BOARD PRESIDENT

The board president holds one of the key positions in the mission-directed governance model, with responsibilities far beyond moderating board meetings. The board president guides the relationships of the board. The board president's responsibilities include the following:

- holding each board member and the board as a whole accountable to follow board policies
- shepherding the board to accomplish its commitments

- directing communication from faculty or constituency to the proper person, rather than placing each request on the board agenda

- effectively moderating board meetings to ensure that the topic is appropriate, that all board members have a voice with no individual dominating the discussion, and that the topic receives appropriate and timely resolution

- working closely with the head of school in preparing the board agenda and keeping each other informed of school issues

- building community and relationships within the board and between the board and administrators

- reporting to the owner

HOW AN INDIVIDUAL BOARD MEMBER MAKES A DIFFERENCE

Under the mission-directed governance model, the individual board member is required to be a member of the team. The individual member's influence must fall within the board's operation as a whole, including its agenda and priorities for action.

Board members who have served under the traditional model may be prone to think that their influence comes through initiating programs and solving problems in response to constituent complaints or desires. Under the mission-directed model, the strength of the school is as a community united to strive toward the same goals. The priorities of the school are made as a community in action; individualism or seeking personal advantages is contrary to a board member's role as part of a larger team.

Each individual board member remains important and can make a difference in the following ways:

1. Each board member offers observations and wisdom as issues are discussed, and votes to influence the direction and operations of the school.

2. A board member may suggest board agenda topics and suggest school programs for evaluation. At designated board meetings the board seeks recommendations from individual members for topics that the board as a whole should consider at future board meetings.

3. If an individual board member has a recommendation for a new policy or an amendment to a present policy, the individual board member submits the written policy recommendation and rationale to the executive committee. Then the executive committee can propose the recommended policy to the board for adoption, put the proposal on a board agenda list that would require the head of school to report, or conclude that the proposal does not merit full board consideration.

4. An individual board member who is concerned that the administrators are not sufficiently enforcing a policy can begin the process that will bring accountability.

5. An individual board member can respond to a parent or employee request—not by trying to solve the complaint, but by explaining the right process to follow for resolution, recommending that the complainant follow the principles of Matthew 18.

BOARD TRAINING

The board can protect the school and operate wisely only as it understands each issue and its relevance for the board. For this reason, the board seeks to inform itself on education and other relevant matters. Board policy may dictate the occasions or topics for discussion, perhaps as part of each board meeting or as a scheduled workshop.

To gain exposure to education trends and issues and to discover what other schools are doing, it is very helpful to have administrators, board members, and teachers attend conferences on education or related subjects. There are likely excellent speakers and presenters of new ideas at specific workshops, but often the greatest benefit mentioned by attendees is the interaction with people from other schools.

Such training should include a review of the essential documents, including the constitution, philosophy, identification of the school's nonnegotiables, and the rationale for their preservation. Board training should include instruction in the theology, philosophy, and mission of the school to ensure that the board members are confident of the school's purpose and the rationale for board goals. Board education should include leadership characteristics expected of board members. It also should include a review of the mission-directed governance model and its rationale. (This book can serve as an excellent training resource.) In addition, at planned intervals, the board should review the board policy handbook and discuss whether any areas need to be reviewed and how consistently policies are being followed.

By having the right board members—prudent people who are committed to the mission of the school and to protecting the nonnegotiables—the school constituency can be confident that the board will give wise leadership in a manner consistent with the school's philosophy

The board governs itself to ensure that it is following the requirements of the owner as defined in the covenant. The board must ensure that future boards will continue such practices. One of the key tasks of the board, then, is to find new board members who will provide the best leadership— people who are committed to preserving the nonnegotiables and are actively advancing the ministry of the school.

BOARD MEMBERS AS TRUSTEES

There are ways to guard against any board member serving as a representative to a special constituency. Before board members officially take office, board policy requires them to sign the code of ethics and commitment, which emphasizes that the board member will serve as a trustee. Signing this code means pledging to adhere to the various practices and positions it contains. Here are just a few of the items included in this code:

- Members pledge to support and advance the mission.
- Members pledge to avoid seeking to change the mission or the nonnegotiables found in the covenant or the board policies.
- Members pledge to maintain the confidentiality of what takes place at board meetings, such as the conversations or positions of individual board members.
- Members pledge to follow board policies, including those concerning communication to school employees and constituents.
- Members declare that they have no conflict of interest financially or relationally with employees or other board members.

It is invaluable to the Christian school to state in a policy that board meetings are closed to the public. Open board meeting can be attractive to boards in which board members represent various constituencies or positions because it allows the constituents to witness that the board member is fighting for their cause. But when the board members are pursuing common goals as trustees, the best practice is to keep the details of its considerations confidential, allowing board members to brainstorm ideas in private. This allows board members to be persuaded by another's perspectives without having to concede a position in public. In the end, the position of the board as a whole is promulgated to the public, but the public does not know the individual position of each board member. This allows a board member to more effectively serve as trustees of the school as a whole.

Policies can also be established that outline a process by which an individual may appear before the board for a specific reason, such as to appeal an administrative decision. The board may also invite consultants or members of the public to give opinions regarding a predetermined topic on some aspect of the school.

FOR REFLECTION AND DISCUSSION

1. In what areas should the board have policies that limit its own authority?

2. What is the authority of the individual board member as a parent, volunteer, or one who listens to a constituent?

3. What do the principles of Matthew 18 have to do with communication within the Christian school community?

4. What are the risks if individual board members are allowed to respond to personal requests from faculty and parents?

5. What are the risks if the head of school is not the consistent communicator of school happenings, including the announcer of board decisions?

6. Why should the majority of the board agree as to what should be on its agenda?

7. What are the advantages and concerns of not opening board meetings to the public?

CHAPTER 13

Selecting New Board Members

Selection of new board members is one of the most critical organizational decisions of any Christian school. It greatly affects the direction of the school.

Earlier we discussed how organizations can shift from their philosophical heritage. A major factor that can determine whether an organization will stay the course or wander off is the selection of board members. This may be a school's most vulnerable point.

The point is that the selection process should do more than approve board candidates for whom there is no objection; rather, the goal is to get the wisest and most committed board members possible.

When boards are pointing out to candidates that service on the board is a great opportunity, there is a great temptation to gloss over the requirements for service. The board should not assume that the candidate understands the school's philosophy and mission. It doesn't want to embarrass candidates or reject an otherwise great person—perhaps a community leader, donor, or good businessperson—on these grounds.

The school board selects candidates for nomination who meet required standards, but the owner actually elects, appoints, or confirms the candidates to serve on the board. It would be easy for the board to approve all candidates with the rationale that the owner (whether an individual or a group) will decide the matter. For the board to shirk its responsibility for due diligence is to make the school vulnerable to future disaster.

It is very important that the board make sure that prospective board members have a strong commitment to the school's philosophical foundations, and the board should be in the position to insist on selecting the strongest candidates. The mission-directed governance model suggests that identifying and soliciting quality board candidates is almost a full-year task. The board establishes a nominations committee and gives it the mandate to seek the best board candidates.

CRITERIA

Both the covenant with the owner and the policies of the board should state minimum qualifications for serving on the board. Such a list should include being a Christian, being committed to the purpose and philosophy of the school, being committed to work within board policies, having one's own eligible children attend the school, and avoiding conflicts of interest. Board members must be clearly committed to preserving the nonnegotiables and enhancing the mission of the school.

There is a misconception that the school board should seek candidates with specific vocational expertise. It is not necessary or in the school's best interest for the school board to select professionals (lawyers, accountants, etc.) as board members. In fact, such selections can be counterproductive. If the board automatically looks to the attorney on the board for legal opinions, it may not seek second opinions or an attorney with different legal expertise. Similarly, selecting a plumber, electrician, or building contractor so that that board member can give professional opinions on facilities can cause conflicts of interest; the board member may expect to get the contract for the new building project. Recognize also that there would likely not be effective accountability of the board member for his or her professional work, whether paid or volunteer. If the board does not fully appreciate the results of the professional, any board expression of dissatisfaction will spill over into the person's relationships with other board members and will likely complicate if not jeopardize that person's future service on the board.

It is fine to select board members without regard to their profession, but there may be a risk in choosing board members because of their profession. The board wants people who understand and support the school's vision, mission, and philosophy. The school wants board members with wisdom who are trustees of the whole school.

SAMPLE POLICIES FOR BOARD MEMBER QUALIFICATIONS

302.7.1. All board members must have a clear testimony of personal commitment to Jesus Christ as their only Savior and Lord and shall personally believe, adhere to, and follow the teachings of the infallible and inerrant Word of God. All board members must agree with the school's statement of faith.

302.7.2. All board members must be actively involved in and regularly attend a local church that adheres to all articles of the Apostles Creed, Athanasian Creed, and Nicene Creed [or some other statement of faith, as appropriate].

302.7.3. All board members must exhibit a lifestyle consistent with that confession, and must not participate in practices that would be considered illegal or considered by the _____ Christian School as immoral or inconsistent with a positive Christian lifestyle (e.g., such as cohabitating without marriage or in a homosexual relationship).

302.7.4. All board members must subscribe to and promote the mission, purposes, and programs that cause _____ Christian School to continue to pursue a biblical worldview.

302.7.5. All board members must be members of the owner group of _____ Christian School unless granted an exception by the board [if the owner is an association].

302.7.6. All board members must enroll all their children who qualify in _____ Christian School. The school board may approve an exception to this policy under special situations.

302.7.7. All board members must give signed agreement to the _____ Christian School board member code of commitment and ethics.

302.7.8. A board member may not have a conflict of interest with members of the school as an employee or a near relative of an employee or near relative of a board member.

302.7.8.1. A near relative is defined as having a connection between persons by blood, marriage, adoption, domestic partnership, or other close personal relationship including cohabitation.

302.7.9. A board member may not be an employee of _____ Christian School (except in a part-time supplemental role such an occasional substitute teacher or coach).

302.7.10. A board member may not be a near relative of a board member with whom there would be overlapping terms of service.

NEW BOARD MEMBER ORIENTATION

Once candidates have been elected and become board members, the new board members should undergo a fairly intensive orientation before they assume their responsibilities. This orientation should include a deeper understanding of the mission-directed model of governance. The orientation should include presentation of the board policy handbook and its use, the role and limitations of the board, the significant issues the board faces, samples of previous head-of-school reports, financial statements, the basics of parliamentary procedure, and other information to help new board members be contributing members. Board policy may invite new members to attend one or two board meetings as observers before actually taking office.

CULTIVATING POTENTIAL BOARD MEMBERS

The board should establish a program to cultivate potential board members. The first step is to identify potential board members. These might include those who were previously nominated but not elected. In addition, there may be inquiries from parents or members of the owner group who are interested in serving. The board could invite such people to learn about the criteria and process for serving on the board. The board could periodically hold informational workshops regarding the school's mission, purpose, and governance, or distribute appropriate literature to potential board members with an opportunity for later discussion.

Under the mission-directed governance model, the board acts as a whole— as a team of people who will guide the direction of the school through the leadership of the head of school. The positive, creative, and optimistic characteristics of the mission-directed governance model that advance the ministry often attract and motivate the best people to serve on the board.

A PROCESS FOR NOMINATING NEW BOARD MEMBERS

How will the present school board be accountable to the owner to ensure that candidates meet the required standards and to determine who will best serve the board at this time? The nominations committee guides the process for determining board candidates. The intention is to have school board membership be seen as a position of respect and desirability. The process begins in early fall by trying to find as many interested people as possible.

The nominations committee invites the owner, general constituency, staff, and board to identify potential candidates. It sends potential candidates a cover letter inviting them to learn more at an informational meeting. At this meeting they are given testimonials from present board members and a packet of information. This packet includes general school promotional materials and information regarding the school's philosophy, the role of the board, the school's long-range plan, the school's governance model, estimated time commitment for board members, and the minimum requirements for serving.

Potential candidates should clearly understand the school's covenant and the founding beliefs that are to be protected, as well as the mission statement and what is to be promoted. This gives potential candidates time to pray, reflect, discuss the possibility with others, and consider the calling. A little later, a member of the nominations committee sets up a conversation with potential candidates to answer questions about the ministry of the school, the board's role, and the limitations of individual board members.

Before being presented to the owner, each candidate should be interviewed by the board as board policy requires. This interview clarifies the candidate's interest, motivation, understanding of the philosophy of the school, and vision for the school; it confirms that the candidate meets the minimum requirements and is a good match with the board. The interview makes explicit the need for the board member to be a trustee rather than a representative of some group or with an agenda to change some issue. The exchange verifies that there is no conflict of interest.

It is worth repeating that the selection process should do more than approve board candidates for whom there is no objection; rather, the goal is to get the wisest and most committed board members possible. The board's strategy is to have more candidates who qualify than there are board openings. The board will select only a limited number of the best candidates to submit to the owner for election.

The covenant with the owner prohibits submission of board candidates at the owner meeting, because there has not been time to ensure that the candidates meet the minimum criteria established by the owner and because names that are raised from the floor may be based on the hope that the person backs or opposes a specific issue. The owner elects board members from among the candidates proposed by the board.

The members of the school board executive committee and the head of school will give the newly elected board members a more thorough orientation to board issues and processes.

FOR REFLECTION AND DISCUSSION

1. What are the minimum requirements to serve on your school board? How do you know what these requirements are?

2. How does the board guarantee that all candidates meet the minimum requirements?

3. Why is it important that new board members be knowledgeable and committed to protecting the nonnegotiables as well as advancing the mission?

4. What is the process by which new board members are oriented to board processes and issues?

5. Why is it important that the board candidate not be motivated by trying to change a specific program or by pushing a specific agenda?

CHAPTER 14

The Effective Use of Committees

The board's use of committees can be a delicate subject. We discussed earlier the risks that can come with board standing committees, including erosion of the authority of the board and head of school. Committees also tend to diminish accountability and eliminate the possibility for change. Determining the agenda for board committees should be initiated by the board; committee agendas should not be determined by the committees themselves.

STANDING COMMITTEES UNDER THE MISSION-DIRECTED MODEL

If the board does decide to establish a standing committee, the board should also establish policies that state the committee's purpose and mandate. Such a standing committee exists to serve the board; it is not a replacement or a competitor. The standing committee is not compelled to meet on a regular basis and does not have to develop a rationale for its existence, and the board establishes its agenda and priorities. The mission-directed model suggests the following three standing committees:

1. EXECUTIVE COMMITTEE

The executive committee has the following tasks:

- Conduct the evaluation of the head of school and recommend to the board whether to renew the head of school's contract and whether there should be conditions placed with the contract. The board as a whole must decide whether to approve the executive committee's recommendation.

- Plan board in-service training and board education as determined by policy.

- Monitor and lead discussions at board meetings or workshops as the board evaluates whether it is following its own policies.

- Handle emergency issues only if the full board cannot meet.

- Handle confidential issues such as doing the preliminary work if there is a challenge to remove a board member or a legal or moral accusation against the school head.

Typically, the executive committee is composed of the board officers. It should be made up of board members who are highly trusted and influential. As with all committees, the board should establish policies that define and control the executive committee's role. The executive committee is not the inner circle that decides issues and then gives its conclusions to the remainder of the board to rubber-stamp.

2. NOMINATIONS COMMITTEE

The task of the nominations committee is to find the best candidates to serve on the school board. These candidates must meet all of the qualifications established by the covenant and the board policies, be committed to the philosophy and mission of the school, and be ready to be trustees under the mission-directed governance model.

3. FINANCE COMMITTEE

Financial stability is critical for the school. The board has fiduciary responsibility for the school. The finance committee reviews the detailed financial records to ensure that the business office and head of school are adhering to the board's financial policies with satisfactory results. The committee reports to the board regarding the general financial fitness of the school. The board will also apply additional measures for maintaining financial health, such as authorizing a financial review or audit of the school's records, or it may recommend to the board new policies regarding financial processes or investments.

By approving the budget, the board authorizes the head of school to carry out tasks within board policies and within that approved budget. The finance committee's role therefore must be defined and limited by policy. The committee should not take over administrative responsibilities and (consequently) eliminate the school head accountability. The committee does not meet to approve specific purchases or second-guess expenditures that are given to the administration by budget or policy.

The school head will find it helpful to submit to the finance committee an early draft of the proposed budget for the committee's advice. This will ensure detailed discussion, but will also provide support to the school head when the first draft is presented to the board. The finance committee makes recommendations, but only the board as a whole may approve the budget.

Financial reports specified by board policies should be included in board packets, and complete financial material should be available to the entire board. Assuming the administration is operating within budget and following established procedures, the board typically needs to devote only a small amount of time at a board meeting to the current financial report.

Unless there is a recommendation for policy change, the head of school is out of compliance with a policy, or there is some financial crisis, the board may not need to go over the details of each financial report. The board is to consider the big picture, such as ensuring that revenue and expenses are meeting budget. The board may wish to place specific proposals on a future board agenda for full-board discussion or may designate the head of school to submit a report.

AD HOC COMMITTEES

There still will be times when the board decides it cannot adequately discuss a thorny issue at a board meeting. Sometimes the issue is too complicated and requires too much analysis or sifting through a great deal of material. The board may find it helpful to assign a group to study and recommend action on such issues.

Ad hoc committees are formed to accomplish a specific task, often with a designated deadline to report to the board. The committee is disbanded when the assigned task is accomplished. These committees help prepare issues for board discussion, but the board makes the final decisions. An ad hoc committee typically defines the issue, prepares a list of topics to be considered, gathers relevant background information, perhaps clarifies possible approaches to resolution, and lists pros and cons with a rationale for each. This gives the board the appropriate information for a profitable discussion and the ability to make a decision and formulate policy.

Ad hoc committees address strategic questions and issues related to the broader school community rather than specific operations or processes. Examples of ad hoc committee issues include the following:

- The feasibility of adding a high school to the elementary and middle schools

- Possible amendments to the covenant

- The feasibility of and process for establishing an endowed foundation for the school

- Long-range options for generating revenue from sources other than tuition

There may be other occasions when the board desires to consider an issue in more depth, especially in response to a head-of-school report. In such cases, the board may assign an ad hoc committee to study whether new policies are needed.

Such ad hoc committees generally are composed of board members and the head of school. Board ad hoc committees rarely involve a staff or external member. Board committees should not do the work of the head of school or staff members. The board may ask others to attend or contribute perspectives as consultants and advisors, especially if they have relevant experience, such as financial, legal, real estate, or construction expertise. The board should also ensure that no members or advisors are placed in a conflict of interest. Committee members who are not members of the school board should not serve as voting members; board members are the only ones who have been elected by the owner to represent the school. The authority and role of the board and of the head of school must be maintained.

HEAD-OF-SCHOOL COMMITTEES

Rather than forming a board ad hoc committee to gather information regarding most school issues, the board will require the head of school to provide information in a report. The head of school may establish various ad hoc committees to assist with the report—for example, to study a particular issue or to help the head of school evaluate a school program. The agenda of the committee is determined by the head of school, and the committee may be composed of staff and community members. As with board ad hoc committees, the agenda and duration and make-up of the committee is not determined by the committee itself; for head-of-school committees, these decisions are made by the head of school.

THE EFFECTIVE USE OF COMMITTEES

This kind of committee is the main way faculty and staff make major contributions to the school program. Examples of reasons to form an ad hoc committee under the leadership of the school head could include the following:

- to generate ideas for accomplishing specified goals (e.g., to develop more educationally relevant and effective field trips)

- to help a faculty member develop an idea or proposal for instructional improvements

- to review some aspect of the school in response to a faculty or staff request

- to study and make recommendations related to school climate

At the discretion of the head of school, ad hoc committees may involve teachers, department heads, or a combination of faculty and staff who are knowledgeable of and affected by a specific decision. The committee may generate a recommendation for the head of school to bring to the board or to initiate an action or event. For example, a committee can be useful for planning and organizing the school's auction or golf tournament.

FOR REFLECTION AND DISCUSSION

1. What is the difference between a standing committee and an ad hoc committee?

2. What are the advantages and risks of having standing committees?

3. How can the role of each standing committee be limited so that it does not speak for the board?

4. How would you decide whether a specific issue should be handled by a board ad hoc committee or a head-of-school ad hoc committee?

PART THREE

Advancing the Mission
of the School

CHAPTER 15

Governance of Student Learning

The mission of the Christian school is usually expressed in terms of student outcomes. Because of this necessary link between student learning and the school's mission, and because the board is accountable to the owner for accomplishment of the mission, board oversight of student learning must be a high priority of governance.

There is an incorrect and dangerous assumption in many schools that the board should not to be involved in oversight of curriculum. Perhaps the exception is the board's interest in how students perform on academic tests. But if the mission states that the purpose of the school is to develop followers of Christ as Savior and Lord, the board must hold the school head accountable for the purposeful design of the curriculum. The mission should also drive cocurricular offerings and general school operating policies.

Too often the assumption is that student learning is the exclusive domain of the teachers, and the role of the board is to provide financial stability, good facilities, and other resources. It is time the board takes responsibility to ensure that the right student learning takes place.

Under the mission-directed governance model, the board has oversight of student learning. The board, school head, and faculty have distinct roles and responsibilities. The board must have oversight on whether what students learn is consistent with the school's mission. The faculty members are responsible for when and how students learn. The school head has responsibility for organizing and coordinating the curriculum with the faculty to ensure that there is evidence of the expected results. The school should be looking at the curriculum from the perspective of what should be the purposeful influences that will shape the students' understanding and skills. In this sense the curriculum should be consciously student-centered.

Under mission-directed governance model, the mission intentionally focuses student learning. This opens the possibility of deliberately developing what the school should philosophically advance, allowing the school to design a purposeful, holistic, comprehensive, schoolwide education plan. Under the mission-directed governance model, school leadership intentionally identifies what students should learn and pursues what the school must do to provide that training. The goal is to make the mission a unifying center that deliberately penetrates and permeates the deepest areas of student learning, that incorporates all subject areas, and that coordinates throughout the years of school training.

To ensure that the curriculum is holistic and comprehensive with biblically based principles integrated throughout, the mission-directed governance model recommends an intentional approach to develop a biblically based curriculum. This involves articulating a curricular plan that is founded on the purpose stated in the school's mission. This educational plan is consciously developed to follow a sequence from philosophy and mission to a schoolwide comprehensive curricular scope and sequence to lesson plans. After these steps, the school considers textbooks or other resources (such as field trips and practical experiences) that will assist the educational process. This takes much more thought and work, but the end product will give better results. This strategy of developing curriculum establishes the school's philosophy, identifies the essential components and worldview perspectives, weaves these concepts into a scope and sequence of courses and lessons, and evaluates textbooks and other resources on the basis of the contribution they make to the curricular plan.

Whole-life Christian discipleship acknowledges that all of life and all relationships are claimed for Jesus Christ; therefore, it is important that Christian discipleship curriculum be focused on the liberal arts. By this we mean that the curriculum must touch on every aspect of life. Education is not only for training for a vocation, citizenship, or self-fulfillment. Students must have knowledge of relationships and culture in order to know what to change. They need skills and training in the tools that will allow them to bring the most effective change. Education must extend as far as our responsibilities within the kingdom of God.

Christian education must be more than teaching academic subjects with some Bible verses attached. The curriculum should be integrated and include common philosophical and worldview elements for all grades in all subjects throughout the curriculum—the school's core curricular principles. The core curricular principles state the key components of perspective and worldview that each child should learn, and they are an extension of the mission statement. The board needs to control the core curricular principles if the school is to possess internal integrity and consistency.

Such a comprehensive educational plan must begin by articulating the goals of student learning and the school's formal curriculum, but under the mission-directed governance model the school is additionally able to think about the implications of other educational and operational aspects of the school. For example, the school should also include in its comprehensive plan the influence of field trips, extracurricular clubs and organizations, and school and class performances, displays, and activities. In addition, other areas such as school policies regarding discipline, social interaction, and awards and recognition have a profound educational impact on the student.

The mission-directed Christian school seeks to provide and promote a comprehensive curriculum with programs and experiences designed to cultivate student conviction, commitment, understanding, and skills to serve the kingdom of Christ in all areas of life and throughout life. Such a school will have the following characteristics:

1. There is a focus on student learning with detailed attention to curriculum and educationally supportive experiences.

2. Growth in discipleship happens within and for community. Education should include relationships and networking with family, church, friends, and the local and world communities, especially with those who can help the school train young people to serve the kingdom. Such education will prepare students for works of service in whatever area God calls them to.

3. The student is to have a kingdom understanding and commitment that will be carried out in thought and action.

4. The school is committed to being a living example of this educational community; it should provide a wide network of service opportunities.

THE ROLE OF THE BOARD

What do board members know about education anyway? Shouldn't all educational matters be in the hands of the faculty? Teachers are usually fairly independent in what they teach. The usual limitation is that they have to follow a particular textbook series. In most Christian schools there is little accountability in what the teacher actually teaches. Teacher evaluation is usually centered on classroom management and teaching style. To reinforce teacher autonomy in course content, some schools (particularly colleges) go so far as to have two boards. One board regulates the school budget, building projects, and the like; a second board goes by some other name such as the faculty council. This self-regulated and unaccountable faculty body is the group that determines the curriculum and other educational matters. This totally unregulated independence is precisely the structure that permits the school to begin a philosophical drift.

The point here is that the board should control the principles and ends of curriculum development. Under the mission-directed model, the board is responsible to the owner, students, parents, and teachers to ensure that what students learn is consistent with the school's philosophy and mission. The board provides the vision that unites the school community and the educational purpose, with the goal of developing a curriculum that infuses a Christian worldview, perspective, and application.

Under this model, the board controls and determines the schoolwide position on the purpose and goals of education and the philosophical and worldview perspective that will be taught to the students. The mission statement establishes the purpose of the curriculum and guides its content. The school board will take a position on the goals and the overarching comprehensive blueprint of the curriculum. The grand design is not left up to a textbook company, an individual teacher, or even a faculty council. The board will also establish policies that give clear expectations, standards of measurement, and accountability that apply to the education offered.

Board governance of student learning and curriculum includes the following:

1. The board sets the core curricular principles that are to be the focus of educational goals centered on student learning as presented in the school's mission statement. Identification and articulation of what should be the core curricular principles can be an assignment given to the school head to work through with the faculty and to present to the board for approval or modification.

2. The board requires the school head to give leadership to faculty to develop a holistic, comprehensive curricular plan that will accomplish the core curricular principles.

3. The board requires the school head to give leadership to faculty to

develop ways to measure the degree to which the core curricular principles are being learned and applied by the students. (This is a different requirement than declaring what teachers are teaching.) This will provide the school with information to commend areas of strength and identify those areas that need improvement.

CORE CURRICULAR PRINCIPLES

The purpose of the core curricular principles is to ensure that student learning addresses the following questions:

1. What are the differences between the Christian religion and worldview and the perspective of other religions and philosophies? Students should be able to distinguish the basic differences between Christianity and other formal religions and cults. Students also should be familiar with and distinguish the differences between Christian philosophical approaches and other philosophies, especially prominent philosophies such as scientism and relativism.

2. What are the essential sources of truth? Students should at least be able to identify that Jesus is the Word incarnate. They should know the Bible is God's inspired, infallible, and inerrant Word by which we understand God, His created reality, the Fall, salvation, and God's will for our lives. Students should know acceptable methods of interpreting and applying the Bible. Students should know that God reveals Himself through creation.

3. What are the essential relationships between God, human beings, and the world? Students should know that creation is good, belongs to God, and continues to be under God's providence and care. Human beings were created in the image of God and are responsible for bringing all relationships under the authority of God. Students should know about the Fall and how sin affects every human activity and relationship, including our intellect, will, decisions, and emotions. Finally, students should know the basic meaning of redemption by God's grace—that the death and resurrection of Jesus Christ on the cross paid for the sins of those who believe in Christ, and that the Holy Spirit empowers believers to live lives of service in gratitude. The student should know that we all are to give thanks to God by loving God above all and our neighbor as ourselves. God continues to

love and care for all of creation. The redemption achieved by Christ affects all relationships, including our relationship with creation. Each Christian is part of the body of Christ, the Church, and is called to faithfully grow in Christian maturity by actively attending and participating in a local Christian church community. The student should know that each Christian is called to mature personal faithfulness as well as to works of service that bring unity, justice, righteousness, and reconciliation to all relationships.

4. What are the implications for discernment, critical thinking, and decision making? Every student is to grow in the ability to discern the faith assumptions that underlie individual and community decisions. The struggle between right and wrong affects all relationships and calls for both personal and corporate discernment.

5. What are the implications for personal lifestyle and for service in the home, church, and community? Every student is to be equipped with the vision and skills for bringing positive change to culture and to all relationships for the advancement of the kingdom of God. Students are to be prepared for works of service to bring justice, mercy, righteousness, and reconciliation to the society and culture.

See the appendix for a more detailed list of sample core curricular principles, with biblical support.

THE ROLE OF THE TEACHER

What, then, is the role of the teacher? The mission-directed governance model appears to be a top-down authoritarian model. Perhaps there are advantages to having the board and the head of school working together, but what are the contributions of the teachers? After all, they are the trained experts in education.

It is true that the mission-directed governance model mandates a great deal of board oversight over the philosophical aspects of the school program. The board coordinates all aspects of the school so that they are consistent with the school's philosophy and contribute to the school's mission. The board's governance responsibility is to ensure that teachers have the same focus and vision. Once the board is assured that the teachers agree with the essential faith positions and understand the mission, direction, curriculum, and the leadership structure, the teachers are then freed to confidently teach and participate with their expertise within those boundaries.

Teachers must teach within the larger scope and sequence and the core curricular principles. The individual teacher should not be an independent curriculum strategist, autonomously determining what is to be taught in an individual classroom at a specified grade level for a specific course of study. Curriculum development needs to be a team effort, with the insight of the educational community centered on the common vision. The classroom is not the teacher's kingdom.

Developing the curriculum is a central task assigned to the head of school, who may assign leadership to a curriculum director, but obviously curriculum development is dependent on and involves the whole faculty. The teacher's responsibility is to help identify what is appropriate in the scope and sequence and the factors that contribute to the master plan. The teacher also designs the specific lessons and then practices the best teaching strategies to ensure that the philosophical and educational goals are met. A major advantage to teachers under the mission-directed governance model is that they now have freedom to develop and coordinate their instruction so that all aspects of student learning are an extension of the school's mission. They can do this without the board or a committee interfering with the specifics of their lesson development.

Under the mission-directed model, teacher ideas and observations typically are solicited through academic departments, grade-level teams, teams formed to consider specific issues, and personal conversations. Under the leadership of the head of school, teachers are involved in forming the scope and sequence of the curriculum, articulating their department philosophy, and determining department goals. They develop the criteria by which to evaluate textbooks and other class resources. It is important to emphasize that the philosophy determines the course of instruction. Textbooks are a resource that must complement what is being taught; these resources do not determine the curriculum.

ACADEMIC AND LIFESTYLE FREEDOM

One reason it is important to dissect and clarify the roles of board and teacher is that this will determine if and when the teacher can ever teach something that may be controversial. Must the teacher always submit to the cultural assumptions of the school constituency? For example, what would be the school's reaction if a teacher challenged students to consider various Christian approaches to such issues as sexual orientation, racial discrimination, gender identity, the debate between creation and evolution, or the reasons why some vote for a candidate from a political party that most members of the school community oppose? Should the school extend some protection for academic freedom?

The case for faculty academic freedom is that teachers need to present and pursue truth that may challenge some of the traditions or beliefs held by the school or constituency. The board is expected to guarantee academic freedom for the teacher so that the teacher's employment is protected from upset major donors, board members, or other influential people. However, in our culture, academic freedom is considered a sacred right, often accompanied by tenure, so that the teachers can teach whatever they believe, whether or not it coincides with the positions of the school. How can the school protect its core positions while allowing teachers to confidently teach even if they challenge solidly ingrained traditions? Should the board place limits on what is taught? What should be the relationship between the philosophy of the school and the freedom of the teacher to pursue truth that may challenge dearly held assumptions of the school?

If the school seriously wants to educate, then students should understand positions that oppose the commonly held beliefs of the organization and positions that oppose Christian beliefs. Education is to be more than indoctrination or propaganda. Remember, the curriculum and related student learning strategies are designed to teach the student truth and disciple the student to Jesus Christ, with a worldview and skills that involve changing the world to bring all relationships and culture under the authority of Jesus Christ. If the teacher cannot enthusiastically and consistently teach this, there should be a parting of the ways. Actually, the place to begin is for the board to establish written policies that state the school's important nonnegotiable positions of belief and lifestyle expected of employees. All employees must willingly agree to teach and comply with these requirements.

In some schools teachers readily agree to teach from the perspective adopted by the school, but problems continue to appear. Experience shows that there will continue to be problems between the school and a teacher or professor. A common situation is that while the school requires the teacher to sign a statement of belief, this commitment is limited to theological positions such as those found in the Apostles Creed or other doctrinal confessions. In addition, the agreement may require the teacher to pledge to adhere to certain personal lifestyle matters. However, problems between teacher and school rarely arise with a direct challenge to a theological position; rather the debates center on the teacher's interpretation of biblical principles and the suggestions to students as to how those principles are to be applied to society, culture, and personal life. What is lacking is an agreement on the school's philosophy and mission. It is recommended that school contracts require the instructor's agreement with the school's philosophy, mission, core curricular principles, and nonnegotiable positions.

If the board has specific interpretations that it insists its employees hold and teach to the students, these should be stated by the board in policies so that all know the expectations before signing an employment contract. For example, a school may have specific teachings it expects to be consistently taught to students such as the creation process, the second coming of Christ, baptism, as well as current social issues such as abortion, the family, and human sexuality.

Is it even legal to limit a teacher's or other employee's academic and lifestyle freedom? Check with your attorney or accreditation agency, but most conditions between the school and an employee or between the school and the parent are based on contract law. As long as the conditions are explicit and the two parties agree on the conditions of employment or student enrollment, such requirements will usually be supported by law.

Under the mission-directed governance model, both the board and faculty have appropriate but separate roles in determining curriculum. The board limits its role to concentrating on the school's mission, overarching documents, and consequent policies. The board holds the head of school accountable to ensure that the curriculum is consistent with the mission. The board remains separated from the daily decisions and details of curriculum formation. Those trained in education design the curriculum, courses, and lessons, and practice the art and craft of teaching.

FOR REFLECTION AND DISCUSSION

1. Why shouldn't an individual teacher independently determine the curriculum for his or her own grade level or course and consequently choose a textbook to go with it?

2. Describe the role of the board and why it should have oversight and influence on the curriculum even though board members may not be trained educators.

3. Describe the role of teachers and why and how they should be accountable to the board.

4. What are the core curricular principles of your Christian school?

5. To what extent should teachers have academic freedom to teach what they think is true, even though it may challenge the traditions or thinking of the school?

CHAPTER 16

Mission-Directed Curriculum Design

As has been said throughout this book, one of the foundational assumptions of the mission-directed governance model is that the whole organization is to be in alignment with the mission. The board's oversight is not limited to financial considerations. It is appropriate and necessary for the board to have governing oversight not only of student learning and the curriculum but also of extracurricular activities, auxiliary organizations, and decisions regarding admissions, employment, student discipline, and other aspects of school life. The board guides these areas by policy and reliance on the school head rather than by direct board or committee involvement. The purpose of this chapter is to show how the curriculum, student learning, and related aspects of the school can be linked to the mission.

CURRICULUM OVERVIEW

The school must determine the essential elements and characteristics of each curricular program that is taught by each department—and whether there even should be academic departments. It must determine the appropriate grade levels at which these various elements will be introduced, reinforced, and taught for mastery learning. This ensures that teaching continues appropriately from one grade level to the next. The depth and breadth of course content is called the "scope" of the curriculum. Determining the appropriate grade levels at which the content is to be taught and in which order it is to be taught is called the "sequence." Thus, the common phrasing of curriculum emphasizes the "scope and sequence" of what is taught. The specific curricular element students should learn is known as the "standard."

Following a traditional academic curriculum, many states and national professional organizations list standards for most academic subjects. This means that schools may use these standards for determining the scope and sequence of the curriculum—what is to be taught at each grade level in mathematics, social studies, English, and so on. For example, a state standard may indicate that at a specified grade level for United States history, the student is to know a list of named key persons and their influence on the American Revolution. Or a state standard may indicate

CURRICULUM DEVELOPMENT FLOW CHART

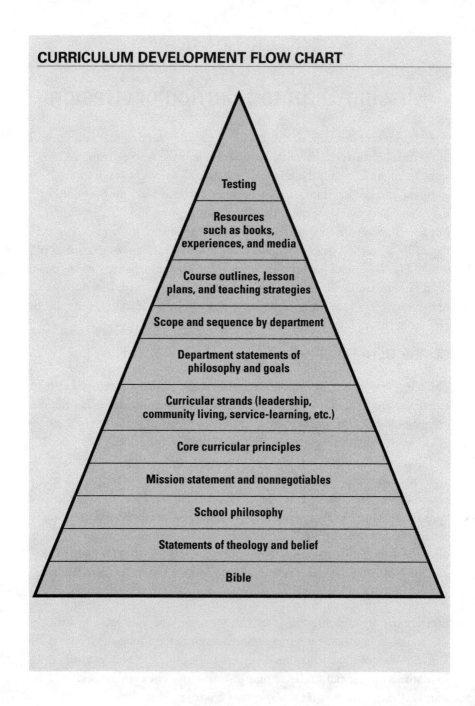

Testing

Resources
such as books,
experiences, and media

Course outlines, lesson
plans, and teaching strategies

Scope and sequence by department

Department statements of
philosophy and goals

Curricular strands (leadership,
community living, service-learning, etc.)

Core curricular principles

Mission statement and nonnegotiables

School philosophy

Statements of theology and belief

Bible

when students are to understand long division. Or a state standard may indicate expectations for student writing and grammar.

How can the board be confident that the academic elements are taught from the school's philosophical perspective and designed to achieve the school's mission? In our example of social studies, we immediately notice that what is missing is a biblical perspective. These academic standards miss the context that is defined in the core curricular principles. The Christian school needs to instill a Christian worldview and perspective for each academic subject. How does the school's philosophy find its way into these subjects?

We have discussed how the board oversees the school's philosophy and mission. By policy the board states the core curricular principles that delineate the perspective the board expects the teachers to consistently teach throughout all subject areas. How is the school head to lead teachers to integrate the subject area concepts with the core curricular principles? The school's focus is on nurturing students to grow in discipleship—equipped with vision, understanding, discernment, and service—in order to renew all relationships and culture to be under the authority of Jesus Christ. This means that the academic subjects must have their purpose and direction linked with the mission. A mission-directed curriculum can be developed by following a step-by-step process such as the following:

STEP 1: DEPARTMENT PHILOSOPHY

The teachers must connect the subject matter to producing the kind of student identified in the mission statement.

A way to begin is to gather the faculty of each subject area for a workshop. The leader says, "Imagine we are reorganizing the school and have decided that the Christian school should teach only the Bible and Christian music. The board thinks your department is fluff, so your subject area will be eliminated unless you can demonstrate to the board how your subject is necessary for the school to accomplish its mission."

Each academic department is to write a statement of its philosophy and purpose that justifies its existence in the curriculum by linking that subject area to the development of followers of Jesus Christ who are striving to place all relationships under the authority of Jesus Christ.

Why should this course of study—such as science, computer education, or art—not be considered fluff and irrelevant for this Christian school? Perhaps one would defend teaching the traditional subjects because it is necessary to get a job. However, that doesn't provide the rationale as to why these subjects should be taught in this *Christian* school.

The point of this exercise is to reinforce the concept that the purpose for teaching must be rooted in the school's mission. The rationale for whole-life discipleship is that math, history, music, and physical education are to be taught because the students who will change the world need the understanding, perspective, and skills provided by this curricular area in their toolbox. In addition, the students must master these subjects in order to get a job, but the purpose of getting a job is to meet their obligation to take responsibility for family, church, and community.

The faculty involved in each subject area must reach a consensus as to how that curricular area contributes to making effective followers of Christ who will change the world. Each department should determine its part in giving the student information, perspective, and skills regarding who the students are and how to analyze our society and culture in preparation for the future. Each curricular area is to designate what is to be taught within the context of vision, a Christian worldview (creation, fall, redemption, restoration), discernment, and service.

Perhaps the following suggestions can be used as a starting point for identifying how each department can contribute to producing whole-life disciples:

- *Bible and religion.* The Bible is God's revelation of Himself and of His will for our lives. We must read and study the Bible as the actual Word of God and be prepared for obedience and life change. The school must teach Bible content, themes, and acceptable principles of Bible interpretation and application. The student should understand how the Bible applies to each of the subject areas. The school should also discuss biblical approaches to religion, philosophy, and worldview in contrast to alternatives to biblically based worship and thinking.

- *Church.* The student should be knowledgeable on the church and its purpose, as well as the church's witness and involvement, both positive and negative, in societies and cultures throughout the ages as well as understanding its calling for believers today.

- *Science.* The created world communicates a great deal about God. We understand how sin affects the study of science even though it proclaims that it provides objective truth outside of God. God appointed us stewards and caretakers of creation, we are to maintain and subdue it to glorify God and help our neighbor. Science can provide opportunity for self-serving manipulation for our own profit without consideration of others or the long-range implications of our actions; it can also provide tools of stewardship in understanding and managing the created order to give glory to God and to love our neighbor.

- *Mathematics.* Besides showing the divine nature and power of God, math is a critical tool needed to transform society and culture. We also see sin linked with math in the manipulation of statistics. Mathematics contains the power to destroy and distort truth. The graduate of the Christian school needs to have the perspective and skills to use mathematics as a tool to serve the kingdom of Christ.

- *Physical education.* Our bodies are temples of the Holy Spirit. We have the responsibility to be healthy and to help others maintain health. Society judges the value of individuals by their outward beauty and physical prowess. Many people with eating disorders are attempting to achieve what they perceive to be the culturally accepted shape. Others have rejected the body as part of the Christian life by practicing asceticism and denying the body its rightful nourishment. We need to explore and test the culture's view of health, recreation, and leisure.

- *World languages.* World languages help us communicate with our neighbors, whether in the house next door or in another country. Language provides the basis of understanding, communication, and relationship-building. In our culture, world language training is often pursued to help us enjoy our travels to another country or to help us do business with the people of that country. While these are legitimate reasons, proficiency in world languages also allows us to relate lovingly as God's representatives to other people and cultures.

- *Social studies.* We explore human relationships, past and present, and the blessings of living as citizens of God's kingdom. We are allowed to learn about our own culture and the culture of others. We can readily see the effects of people who do or do not apply biblical principles within society. Social studies help us develop a sense of perspective as to place and time, with insights into the dominant cultural principles that guide people's thinking and habits. Social studies help us understand the consequences of how a civilization practices the principles of service, justice, and stewardship.

- *Language arts.* Language is a gift of God to communicate with Him and others, which includes listening, reading, writing, speaking, comprehending, and interpreting.

- *Fine arts.* Created in the image of God, we are designed to explore and express our experiences and beliefs through art, music, fashion, media, and drama.

- *Technology.* Technology is a tool that can help us extend learning and service, especially in diverse and global settings. Technology is not the all-powerful tool that holds the key to all understanding.

- *Economics and business.* The student must be taught to make wise choices that will promote stewardship in production and distribution of resources that enhance justice and righteousness.

STEP 2: SCOPE AND SEQUENCE ESSENTIAL GOALS

Following its department statement of philosophy, each department should develop a list of essential goals and worldview characteristics to be taught within the scope and sequence of the subject area. The department scope and sequence should show how these essential characteristics ought to be integrated in each course at each grade level.

STEP 3: DEVELOPING COURSES

The teacher creates lesson plans in light of the general worldview perspective adopted by the school, the core curricular principles, and the academic concepts to be taught that fit into the scope and sequence of the whole curriculum. The teacher is responsible for designing instructional units and lesson plans that will incorporate the standards identified for that class and course. The teacher will incorporate appropriate methods, strategies, and measurement tools that confirm whether the education is successful.

When departments and teachers consider each course of study, the school may ask teachers to answer questions—such as the questions suggested below—to help teachers construct the content and perspective of units and lesson plans as well as hold the teacher accountable to the administrators.

- Why does a person who seeks to bring all relationships under the authority of Jesus Christ need this course? How does this course bring right understanding of the world and culture, right vision toward what the students should strive for, or mastery of a tool that is needed to bring change?

- How does this curricular area equip students to be Christian leaders who will communicate the gospel of salvation in Jesus Christ and bring Christ-centered justice, righteousness, and reconciliation into relationships and culture?

- How does this curricular area enable the student to become aware of opportunities for service, and develop their talents, skills, and interests for service?

- What service experiences does this course require or provide?

- How is this course related to and integrated with other departments and courses so that the student understands the wholeness of life and experience?

- How does this course enable the student to discover criteria by which to discern a Christian perspective and build right relationships?

- How does this curricular area enable the student to understand the results and consequences of discernment and decision making from a Christian perspective as well as from alternative perspectives?

- How does this curricular area enable students to commit to transforming personal and community culture?

STEP 4: ARTICULATION OF THE CURRICULUM

Mapping the curriculum means writing out the scope and sequence for each curricular subject or strand. Curricular mapping involves identifying and defining the content of each strand in terms of the subject and the grade level at which it is to be taught. This description should include the purpose and objectives of what is to be taught along with an explanation of how it is an extension of something already taught or how the topic is an introduction to what will be taught in greater depth at some other time. This also provides an opportunity to describe sample lessons, resources, and educational experiences, projects, and field trips. Thus curricular mapping is designed to be prescriptive—in other words, the map indicates to the teacher what ought to be taught.

Curriculum mapping helps ensure that the teacher is in agreement with the school's expectations of what to teach—the curricular scope and sequence with the standard for each subject. This is more complete than the typical curriculum guide, which may merely give a snapshot describing what is being taught in each course at each grade level as recorded by the teacher. There are computer programs that make this project much easier than placing these ideas in a binder that no one will read. Curricular mapping will ensure that the school is incorporating the essential characteristics into its curriculum, identifying gaps in instruction, and reducing curricular redundancies. Curricular maps will be especially helpful for substitute teachers as well as for new faculty members.

Within the project of curricular mapping, we identify the departments of instruction, their academic content and standards, and their perspective in relation to the core curricular principles. In addition, the school maps the curricular strands it expects to be taught, such as service-learning, components of leadership, whole-life discipleship, living in community, and integration of technology.

FOR REFLECTION AND DISCUSSION

1. Why should Christians participate in a liberal arts education—not just education for the purpose of getting a job and not just the study of the Bible or theology?

2. If your school head were to threaten to cut mathematics because of a claim that it is irrelevant to the mission of the school, how would you explain that it is necessary?

3. To what extent is it helpful to use state or other existing standards to measure academic effectiveness?

4. How can the school design courses that are meaningfully related to the mission of the school?

CHAPTER 17

Governing School Culture and Influences

To most effectively nurture students who are savvy Christians—who understand the world and their commitment to bring all relationships, society, and culture under the authority of Jesus Christ—the school should develop its curriculum to be more than the traditional curriculum used by schools that have a different mission. The board has oversight of the formal curriculum that seeks to nurture the students in understanding each course of study from a biblical perspective. However, there are additional strands of teaching that can be woven throughout the subject area curriculum and the school experience. Let us consider three strands that are important in order to develop the kind of student identified in the mission statement.

1. DISCIPLESHIP WITHIN COMMUNITY

One strand the school seeks to include is nurturing the student to develop the vision of discipleship. In order to be a disciple, the student needs a genuine and personal relationship with Jesus Christ as Savior and Lord. As a disciple, the student seeks to be God-centered, obediently bringing himself or herself and all relationships under the authority of Jesus Christ.

Christian school leaders often mention the following three characteristics when discussing student discipleship:

First, disciples have a spirit of gratitude for salvation—along with a sense of awe and piety in which they learn to love God with obedience and God-centered awareness. The school nurtures gratitude through prayer, Bible study, and other practices that help develop personal holiness.

Second, disciples should develop personal character traits such as self-discipline, integrity, honesty, and truthfulness. Students demonstrate such traits as they take ownership of the activities in which they serve and lead.

Third, disciples should develop a keen sense of discernment and wise decision making. This calls for personal conviction. Students see Kingdom implications in everyday issues, have a sense of right and wrong, and are committed to accept personal responsibility for their actions.

The Christian school recognizes that it is not the only or even the primary community within which disciples are formed. The school should consider the intentional formation of relationships with other disciple-shaping communities. The home, church, and school have the same mandate to produce whole-life disciples. The family is the most influential institution. The school also deliberately seeks to solidify the student's relationship with the church. The church is the one institution that the student should grow with throughout life. The school is an extension of the home and church, not a replacement. Therefore the school should explore ways to build strong ties with the home and church. Without trying to take over the role, authority, or accountability of the home and church, the school can strive to develop strong relational ties and experiences that unite home, church, and school. For example, the school can work with the church to host speakers, workshops, or parent discussion groups on topics such as age-appropriate discipline, traditions, family devotions, suitable entertainment, and student social life expectations.

2. CHANGING SOCIETY AND CULTURE THROUGH SERVANT-LEADERSHIP

A second strand the school should incorporate is calling students not only to love God above all, but also to love their neighbors as themselves. The point here is that if the school has the mission to promote discipleship and leadership, the school must teach these intentionally. The mission-directed model expects these aspects to be deliberate, planned, and measured.

First, students need to understand the realities of the world. This is why the academic subject matter should emphasize creation (what God created the world to be), the Fall (what the world became through sin, and the overwhelming evidence of the Fall), redemption (including not only personal redemption through the sacrifice of Jesus but also God's call to bring justice, righteousness, and reconciliation), and restoration (the recovery of the original intent of creation in the new heaven and earth when Jesus returns). A call to service also comes with the call to be agents of reconciliation by bringing all relationships under the authority of Jesus Christ.

Second, students need to know something about themselves. Each student explores who he or she is—created with particular talents, skills, interests, and gifts. The school can then help by having each student consider where God would use him or her to build His kingdom.

Third, there needs to be training in biblical servant-leadership skills. The school is to apply and bring transformation to the student's life with the expectation that the student will transform his or her relationships and culture. If the purpose of the Christian school is to nurture Christian change-makers, the Christian school should include training in the components of leadership as a purposeful part of the curriculum. Since the school's purpose is to insist on servant-leadership, such training does not require the student to vie to be boss or chair of every committee. Students will be called upon to make godly decisions in their homes, churches, and communities, and many will be asked to take on leadership roles within those arenas. Part of good leadership is being an informed follower and knowing when another leader should be encouraged or challenged. However, students should not automatically shy away from such leadership opportunities either. It is important that students know how to function within a community. It is important for students to learn leadership skills that bring change.

The school can include leadership goals in its curriculum. These aspects can be taught at all grade levels with more complexity. Each student will

1. understand and practice the skills of organization, sequence, detail, and management;

2. provide leadership that prevents quarrels and brings resolution to situations in which there are differences of opinion;

3. deal with emergency, unpredictable, ambiguous circumstances; and

4. initiate a concept that meets a need or takes advantage of an opportunity, make a plan of action, and complete the implementation to produce a practical solution that meets the designated purposes.

General leadership skills include living in community (e.g., understanding roles found within an organization, handling conflict and differences), developing organization skills, and learning to predict and anticipate consequences of decisions. These competencies and skills can be taught in ways appropriate for the grade level. For example, a second-grade teacher may talk about an anticipated field trip to the zoo. The students can discuss the reasons for the trip and how the teacher will know they have accomplished the purpose, such as by having each student name five animals and draw a picture of one. The teacher can introduce when the field trip will take place and what each students will need to plan for to make it successful (e.g., lunch, notebook, camera). They can discuss why they need to stay together and use line leaders, and why they would wear shirts of the same color. The teacher can discuss with the class the possibilities of what they would do if it rains, if someone forgets to bring lunch, or if anyone gets lost. Such training will increase with grade level.

3. PARTICIPATING IN SERVICE-LEARNING

One of the primary purposes of academic studies is to provide Christian change-makers with necessary understanding and skills for successful Christian service. Christian schools can reinforce these principles and offer experiences that will help students learn leadership skills by having students participate in service-learning opportunities.

Service-learning is different from mission trips. Mission trips can be effective vehicles for service-learning; however, mission trips are usually done on a one-time, short-term basis and involve a limited number of participants. Service-learning opportunities are designed to have an impact on other people and develop long-term relationships with them. Service-learning can involve all students at all grade levels. Service-learning involves gaining experiences that transform some aspect of culture or society for real people.

To successfully participate in service-learning, the student must be academically prepared for the experience. The student should be armed with knowledge of the historical, economic, and cultural circumstances that created the need in the first place; they should also learn as much as possible about the people they are going to serve.

The following examples may help in understanding service-learning and may suggest many more opportunities. Most of these can be adapted for various grade levels, integrated into particular subjects or units, and done year after year.

- Sponsor a service dog that is being trained to assist people who have disabilities.

- Plant and care for a garden to raise food for a homeless shelter or food pantry.

- Save coupons that can be used to purchase supplies for another school.

- Play games, make birthday or holiday cards, or perform programs at a retirement center or children's hospital.

- Sponsor an international Christian aid organization for a specific project such as digging a well for clean water.

- Provide after-school tutoring for neighborhood children.

- Sponsor and assist in programs for Special Olympics.

- Partner with a school in another country.

- Develop relationships with students in a younger grade through activities such as reading, performing puppet shows, playing sports, or serving as referees or umpires for their games.

- Provide services for the community such as painting or constructing playground equipment or park benches.

- Meet with and learn from leaders of community social agencies.

- Fill shoeboxes with necessities for homeless people.

THE PLACE OF MEANINGFUL COCURRICULAR EXPERIENCES

The board should insist that all aspects of the school be accountable to the board. This includes cocurricular programs. Christian education does not stop when the student has intellectual comprehension; it also includes what happens outside of the classroom.

Extracurricular clubs and organizations are an important part of a school's offerings. Elementary students engage in special events such as music and art festivals, concerts, interschool contests in spelling, geography, and chess, as well as programs and plays. At the middle and high school levels, such events (especially athletics) typically take on more visibility and time commitment. Specific clubs and organizations are formed to enhance skills and interests (e.g., as student council, debate club, and academic specialties such as science club). There also are organizations that promote opportunities for service, such as the Kiwanis Key Club and National Honor Society.

These are important offerings because they provide enrichment opportunities that are not easily available in the classroom. They enhance discipleship by strengthening skills and talents as well as by providing opportunities to explore new prospects. Extracurricular areas provide the opportunity to apply what is taught in the classroom.

The school's philosophy should suggest programs the school needs to reinforce classroom instruction. This will call for purposeful education that features a balance of such areas as athletics, drama, social activities, field trips, service opportunities, and student clubs and organizations.

It is important to make a special note for clubs and activities that are competitive. This is not the forum to debate the level of competition at various grade levels, but most schools with a middle school and especially a high school program probably have chess clubs, forensic teams, academic competitions, and athletic programs. Scores of books point out the positive effects students can acquire, such as respect for referees, judges, and the opposition; teamwork toward a common goal; self-discipline; recognizing that not all are suited for every sport and every position or activity; how to balance academics with other school activities, home and family obligations, and lifestyle and training expectations; and how to handle the pressure of wins and losses in a Christian manner. The point is that the school must seriously consider the importance of cocurricular programs when thinking about discipleship. These are not areas in which our discipleship goals are put aside. It is incumbent on the Christian school to see these as intentional discipleship areas. Consider the lifetime influence of coaches. The coach is often a personal mentor and has a lasting influence. The coach provides a prime opportunity to model the Christian life. The same is true for leaders in other cocurricular arenas.

MAKING THE CHRISTIAN SCHOOL A LIVING EXAMPLE

The board should be aware of and hold the school head accountable for the school culture. Board policies should ensure that the school operates in ways that are consistent with the mission.

In addition to formal and informal programs, education takes place through example. Actual practices of relationships can model and enhance the growth of Christian disciples. The school must reinforce its leadership training by operating according to the same principles it teaches students.

Here are a few suggestions to stimulate conversations on how school leaders may promote authentically Christian school operations and programs:

Having the school's guiding policies enhance the school's philosophy

The Christian school should do its best to ensure that its policies provide for a safe and orderly community. The school strives to ensure that its policies and procedures are based on biblical principles and promote training for life skills. All categories of policies—such as finance, admissions, facilities, faculty, and expectations for staff— need to be considered. Operational policies and the school climate should give a sense of orderliness, predictability, safety, and affirmation.

A suggested strategy is to have each staff department of the school write a statement of department philosophy. These statements are similar to the curricular department philosophies we covered in a previous chapter. Examples of departments may include maintenance, transportation, food service, business office, and others. The purpose is to ensure that every department recognizes that it is an integral part of the ministry. At a school I was involved with, I was very pleased when the school was being reviewed by an accrediting organization. One of the accrediting team members talked with a person mowing the lawn, a bus driver, and a cafeteria worker. Each employee could explain the mission of the school and how his or her role was important to the success of the ministry.

Developing real relationships in community

The mission-directed governance model is a valuable tool that protects the essential nonnegotiables and promotes positive steps toward achieving the ideal. However, its success depends on the understanding, commitment, integrity, and skill of the people who use it.

The mission-directed governance model provides the opportunity for the school community to unite around a common purpose and mission in which all recognize that they are servants who are sharing, working, and striving to reach common goals. Distinguishing roles and purposes allows the community members to gain a greater respect for each other and the contribution each makes, and also allows the process of decision making to be more predictable and peaceful.

The teachers and staff should be personally committed to Jesus Christ and feel called to their profession. The teaching faculty is trained to teach from a Christian perspective. All employees recognize that they have a responsibility to model Christian ideals and lifestyle. All are living examples of caring, sensitive, whole-life disciples of Christ. They develop loving personal relationships with each other, with students, and with parents.

Discipleship within community also means that students must recognize their responsibility to the larger body. They should develop a greater understanding of purpose, service, and responsibility, along with a sense of humble gratitude for the opportunity to serve as catalysts who bring positive change. The school's goal should be for each student to

- recognize that he or she has been created to live and work in community with others—in the body of Christ and in the world;
- demonstrate individual skills that promote teamwork and communication;
- maintain cooperative relationships with others;
- demonstrate individual skills that promote teamwork and communication;
- show concern for people and attempt to meet the needs of others; and
- intentionally honor bus drivers, custodians, before-school and after-school care providers, office workers, members of auxiliary groups, and others who faithfully serve the school community.

Students should not be passive participants in the school mission. They should be taught the purpose and vision of the school so that they know what unifies their studies. Students should be able to articulate the reason they are in the Christian school. They are the direct beneficiaries of all the personnel, facilities, activities, and history of the school. The mission-directed model attempts to help students receive an education that is purposeful and consistent.

A goal of Christian schools is for students to understand and practice living in community. The student needs to be consciously aware of the principles of Christian living. These principles should be purposefully taught and integrated within the curriculum and school experience. How can the school train students to develop a Christian understanding and the appropriate skills of living within a community?

First, teach biblical principles regarding friendships, family, marriage, church, and community. One example of such a principle of community living is how to resolve disagreements. Most Christian schools teach these within Bible classes or other classes as the topics arise. The suggestion here is that these principles should be articulated and made part of the curriculum throughout all grade levels and subject areas.

Second, help students apply these principles within their present experiences and relationships. The school wants these principles to be actually taught and become part of the operation of the relationships that exist within the school.

These are practical ways in which students become empowered to begin to change their world and their way of relating now, rather than thinking all of their education is for later, when they become adults. The teacher can give a vision of what relationships ought to be.

FOSTERING DISCIPLESHIP THROUGH DISCIPLINE POLICIES

The school's desire to be a living example of a Christian educational community should influence the school's policies for all operations and practices—including policies relating to student discipline.

Living in community will provide many opportunities for the school to consciously call attention to practices that reinforce the school's mission. When these principles are articulated and visible, they can be applied to real-life situations and real people. There are opportunities for students to learn about conflict resolution, conflict prevention, family and church relationships, and future relationships with employers and colleagues.

For example, at the elementary level the school promotes sound social interaction. The playground is part of the Christian school ministry. In fact, the playground may be one of the most important "classrooms." As all of life belongs to Jesus Christ, this includes our recreation, our leisure, and our breaks from work. The playground is where the school can help the students learn to act out what they really believe. It is here that boys and girls can translate their understanding of "love your neighbor as yourself" into actual practice. The Christian school teaches students to live for Jesus. The school wants the children to stand up for what is right, to tell the truth, to be kind to others, and to use proper language. The playground is certainly one place for the student to learn that life is filled with fun. Here is where children can share and cultivate good friendships and learn social skills. Students learn to include others.

But the playground is also a place of disagreements and conflicts. The Christian teacher guides the resolution of problems. Students learn to take turns, to control anger, and to work and play in community. It is here that students learn to put things in perspective and find that perhaps what they thought was a huge problem really isn't so bad after all. On the playground, students learn to share and to resolve social problems. Students can learn how to invite and include others, such as students new to the school, into games and activities. Here students learn to forgive and to recognize that Christians sometimes need to ask forgiveness of others. Your child may have difficulties with other students, but this may be the most important time to have your child in a Christian school. The playground is the Lord's, and so the Christian community members dedicate and pledge their fun and their recess to Christ's service.

These principles of living in community can be taught at the middle and high school levels as well. For example, at the middle and high school level, living in community often takes place informally during breaks, lunch, and social occasions. The school should consciously provide a number of programs and activities for social interaction. These opportunities provide experiences that promote healthy and appropriate relationships with peers and friends. Students can be taught to be aware of the needs of others and to be a listening and helpful friend through a peer counseling program. Students can be coached to provide relational advice within a limited scope and with school counselor knowledge, support, and resources. Such discussion often resolves potential disputes and hurt feelings by following the mandates of Matthew 18.

Other educational opportunities take place at social occasions such as banquets, mixers, and parties. There are sports teams and other extracurricular clubs and organizations based around some common activity. There are occasions for leadership and service projects. The school needs to guide each of these activities with an eye toward developing social relationships and growing Christian leaders.

Student discipline is the application of the principles of living in community. The school should be a community based on Christian principles. It is necessary that each individual help and be helped by the community in maturing as disciples of Christ. There needs to be encouragement when consistency is exhibited and correction when there is inconsistency. Discipline should seek to develop self-discipline, in which students understand and seek to follow biblical principles because they are learning to be disciples of Jesus Christ. Consequently, the school attempts to emphasize many biblical principles for living, not just obedience to authority. Again, Christians should pursue positive discipleship, not just corrective discipline.

School discipline policies should be based on biblical principles. For example, it is important for persons to live responsibly with others. There should be predictable natural consequences to infractions, but not with the intent to humiliate the student. Of course, at times it will be necessary to impose detentions or other actions for repeated infractions against institutional programs, but discipline policies should bring about justice and righteousness rather than merely punishment or deterrence. Discipline policies that address broken relationships between people should be handled in a way likely to encourage repentance and reconciliation.

For example, if a student exhibits a consistent pattern of minor infractions that have accumulated or if the student commits a more serious infraction, how can such a situation be dealt with in a way that helps the student see the impact of that behavior on the whole community? Here is one process that has had success on the middle and high school levels.

- Begin with indefinitely suspending the student.

- Schedule an appointment with the administration for the student and at least one parent.

- At least the day before having this conference, ask the suspended student to write and submit an essay that responds to such questions as the following:

  What should be my character? Why? For what characteristics do I want to be recognized? What examples show I am becoming that kind of person?

  What is the purpose of this school? What kinds of student should be admitted?

What kinds of person should not be allowed to be a student or should be told to leave?

What has been the problem? What are the biblical principles that apply to this situation? What messages have my previous attitude and behavior sent?

Why do I want to be at this school?

What can the school expect as to my attitudes and behavior? What assurances can I give to reassure the school that my future attitudes and actions will contribute to the school community?

How will I make amends for and correct this most recent situation?

• One or more conferences may follow this essay.

Such a process can bring understanding of the problem, repentance, awareness of consequences, and reconciliation. If the student is defiant, unrepentant, or refuses reconciliation, the school may decide not to readmit the student to class. In these worst cases, the parent may find it advisable to find another educational alternative.

FOR REFLECTION AND DISCUSSION

1. Why should Christian schools purposefully incorporate discipleship development?

2. How does your school disciple students?

3. Why should Christian schools purposefully incorporate teaching leadership skills?

4. How does your school prepare students to be leaders who will bring all relationships under the authority of Jesus Christ?

5. Why should Christian schools incorporate service-learning? What should be included in that service-learning training?

6. How can field trips and extracurricular activities, especially competitive programs such as athletics, further the mission of the Christian school?

7. How do a school's discipline practices affect the overall mission of developing disciples?

CHAPTER 18

Governing by Measuring

The school board and the school head need to consider their leadership in bringing changes that will further advance the school toward its mission. However, before the school leaders can make wise and informed decisions regarding the best course of action, they need to have the right information regarding what is the present status and condition of the various areas of the school. Once they have valid and complete information about the condition of the various aspects of the school, then the school leaders can determine a course of action with priorities. What information should the board have?

DECIDING WHAT TO MEASURE

Sometimes it is good to get anecdotal information. Interesting stories are important to include in the school newsletter to let the constituency and families that may potentially enroll their children know that the Christian school positively affects real people. However, for evaluation of aspects of the school, the board should seek to gather measurable information, not just narrative sketches.

Measured information will be more objective than anecdotal information. The board will have a better grasp of strengths and weaknesses and be able to see whether there are trends or fluctuations over a period of time, rather than reacting to a situation in alarm. With measured information, the board is in a better position to target goals and to determine whether there has been improvement. The board will have the information needed to prevent problems rather than waiting for the parents or employees to identify problems. The board can concentrate on advancing the mission and not merely on correcting problems. With measured data, the board is in a position to praise rather than be confined to negative information. Having the right and balanced information will make serving on the board a much more enjoyable experience.

All schools recognize the need to measure student academic results, but if the board has greater aspirations than only academic results and college entrance, then there is more to be measured. What the board assesses shows what the school values and what is the real mission. If the mission is to nurture followers of Christ who will change society and culture to be under the authority of Christ, then the school needs to measure these characteristics as well. In the Christian school, the board needs to insist on measuring the components of what is presented in the mission statement. This is the core reason the school exists, so surely the board will want to know how student discipleship is to be measured, and the board will want to know the results. The board will also want to have information regarding student discipline.

The school should measure characteristics by such methods as testing, evaluation, and measurement for student comprehension and knowledge of the core curricular principles, the practice of service-learning, and growth in Christian leadership. Not all measurement of student performance can be accomplished by paper-pencil or optical-scan tests. Schools need to consider portfolios, journals, and other indices.

Besides having accurate information on student learning, the board needs to know the composition of the school, such as number of students and teachers as well as family ties to local churches. The board will want to know the various school programs designed to help students and the effectiveness of these programs. For example, the school may have programs for students with learning differences, before-school or after-school care, or a lunch program. The board should know what are the extracurricular programs and the purposes they serve. Other aspects of the school to be measured include measuring the competency and skill level of teachers and a host of other characteristics that reveal the school's effectiveness and achievements (e.g., standards for school finances and maintenance of facilities).

STRIVING FOR EXCELLENCE

The head of school calls for excellence in all aspects of the school. Commitment, identification of standards, and accountability are all necessary ingredients to bring about excellence in academics and discipleship and to make the school a living example of discipleship to Jesus Christ. Parents should not be forced to choose between a Christian education and a quality education for their children.

When a Christian school is running well, it is the result of visionary leadership and lots of hard work by many people. Quality is a deliberate choice. Quality is no accident. Sometimes it costs money, but it always requires having clear goals and paying close attention to detail. Quality is producing what the school claims is its purpose. Quality is holding the board, teachers, and students accountable to biblical standards that will be a witness to the community.

MEASURING QUALITY

A significant concern is determining which information is relevant. What do the school leaders identify as quality? How do schools or the constituents define quality? Is quality primarily the mark of student results on academic standardized test scores? Is quality the number of Bible verses students memorize, or students' conformity to teacher demands? What information is relevant? By what standard does the board determine that it can truthfully advertise the school's excellence? Who will use the information, and for what purposes?

With a close eye on the mission, the board, administration, and faculty will need to identify what should be measured, set standards for excellence, and create criteria for determining whether the school measures up to the established standards. The board needs standards by which to measure the degree to which the school is accomplishing its goals.

To wisely pursue the school's goals, the board must have accurate information describing the school's present status. The board must know the present condition of student learning, the effectiveness of the school's programs, and how the school is perceived by various groups.

There are many academic assessments, such as testing for reading, mathematics, science, and even art. However, the school board should approve what is to be tested and approve which tests the school will use.

To assess some aspects of the school that the board wants measured may require the administrator and faculty to develop testing strategies personalized to fit the school's purposes. For example, the faculty will have to prepare measurement strategies for testing the extent to which students understand the core curricular principles.

EVALUATING THE SCHOOL IN PARTNERSHIP WITH OUTSIDE SOURCES

Most schools use a variety of resources from people outside the school to help determine whether the school is meeting accepted criteria. Some hire an accounting firm to conduct periodic financial reviews or audits. There are also reports and certificates from health, safety, and fire inspectors. The board might engage a development company to conduct a feasibility study on whether the community is ready and willing to support a new building project. The board also may consider measuring quality by awards or other recognitions granted by outside professional or civic organizations.

Sometimes comparison is possible with information provided by other schools. For example, schools commonly keep and make publicly available on their website statistics such as standardized test scores, graduation rates, attendance percentages, student retention, and the number of graduates accepted to colleges. However, it is very difficult to make such comparisons accurately. For example, are transportation, books, and extracurricular participation included in the tuition rates? Comparing student test results, even though the test results may be listed on a school's website, is difficult as some schools require all eligible students to take the standardized tests, but some schools require only those students who are expecting to attend a four-year college to take the test.

A most helpful source of external help in determining the heath of the school is an accrediting agency such as the Association of Christian Schools International. Accreditation can be an important aid in promoting quality. Accreditation is recognition by an outside professional organization that a school is meeting professional standards established by that organization.

Accreditation helps in the following ways:

- First, the essential purpose of an accreditation process is to confirm that the school is striving to meet its own mission and philosophy by policy and practice. The intent is that the school will continuously work toward improving its organization, programs, and procedures in accordance with its mission.

- Second, accreditation team visits confirm to the board, faculty, and constituency that many good things are going on and that there are positive results. An accreditation visit will usually conclude its report with a list of commendations. Accreditation results also will likely recommend several items that the school should improve. Accreditation gives assurance to prospective families that they can reasonably expect the school to provide what it promises.

- Third, accreditation gives all associated with the school some insight into how it compares with other schools. Most board members have no other school with which to compare. Perhaps they think of what the school was like when they attended it. Perhaps a board member's children attended a Christian school in another area. Most board members are not acquainted with a broad spectrum of schools with which to compare their school. How can they know whether the school really is competitive in academic results or curricular offerings? Accrediting organizations are able to provide an outside perspective, aided by a team of qualified educators who are usually familiar with scores of other schools.

To discover the opinions of parents and others regarding the school, the board may require the head of school to gather data from within the school community on a number of identified issues and then report to the board. The board may require the head of school to keep information regarding designated aspects of school climate such as relationships between teachers and student, between teachers and school head, and between parents and teachers; what students like most and least about school; and the quantity and severity of student discipline. The board can require that statistics be kept on teacher retention from year to year. It may require the head of school to conduct a school image survey to assess the opinions of parents, faculty and staff, alumni and alumni parents, church representatives, and members of the general community.

The school may develop new measurement tools regarding the extent to which the school is achieving its mission and report the results to the board. For example, the school may develop ways to test and measure the degree to which the students are learning the essential vision and core philosophical principles that underpin the curriculum. See the appendix for a sample of core curricular principles and measurement suggestions.

EXAMPLES OF AREAS OF THE SCHOOL THE BOARD SHOULD REQUIRE TO BE MEASURED

1. Characteristics and composition of the school
   - A history of enrollment for each grade level and the school as a whole
   - The number of students who have left, their reasons for leaving, and the number of new students
   - The number and types of churches student families attend
   - The ethnic diversity of the students
   - Specific financial data
   - Volunteer hours
   - A record of the health and safety of the facilities
   - Reports from accreditation associations
   - Relationship with school owner
   - Number of faculty and staff, characteristics, and qualifications
   - Before-school and after-school care and other such programs
   - Food and nutrition
   - Safety and compliance with government requirements
   - Transportation
   - Area and population from which the school draws or could draw students
   - Socioeconomic, real estate, and ethnic information
   - Number of churches who do or could potentially support the school

2. What the school wants students to learn
   - Student academic progress for various grade levels (determined by general academic tests and/or specific subject testing)
   - Student understanding and application of core curricular principles (whether students are growing in discipleship, vision, understanding, discernment, and service)
   - Student understanding and application of core curricular principles (whether students are growing in discipleship, vision, understanding, discernment, and service)

- Student understanding of worldview
- Student discipline and behavior, character, motivation, experience, service, and more
- Graduates accepted to colleges or other postsecondary institutions

3. Indicators of school programs designed to teach the students

- Programs for students with learning differences
- Extracurricular offerings
- Chapel and other opportunities for worship
- School image survey (observations of parents, faculty and staff, and selected students regarding satisfaction, effectiveness, and direction of the school)

DASHBOARD INFORMATION

When considering measurement, it is helpful for the board to get information at two levels. The board will want access to more extensive and deep evaluation on specific topics, such as the details of the school's financial status, academic test scores, and other programs that have a significant influence on the overall direction of the school. But it is also helpful for the board to have access to quick checkpoints that indicate whether closer attention is needed. These indicators may alert the board to a problem that requires a more in-depth analysis, just as a warning light on a vehicle dashboard may alert the driver that the oil is low. For example, the board may specify that it is to receive an alert when any areas of finances are outside specified limits, such as tuition receipts being below a specific threshold. The board should establish policies that list the dashboard topics and the thresholds that will trigger an alert. These quick, summary statistics may indicate a need for analysis, or they may confirm that everything is normal.

SCHOOL IMAGE SURVEY

In addition to measurement of the items listed above, the board will likely be interested in the observations of parents, students, and staff regarding how well the school is achieving its mission. The board can require the head of school to conduct a school image survey periodically and report the results to the board. The survey asks parents, faculty, students, and others from the school community for their observations on various aspects of the school—on a graduated scale from poor to excellent. Written comments also are solicited. Items on the survey could include the following:

- How effectively the school is moving in the direction of its mission statement
- Whether the school takes seriously its calling to be Christian
- Whether the school provides a safe environment
- Whether the respondent is seen as an important part of the school community
- How the respondent rates the school's curricular offerings
- How the respondent rates the school's extracurricular offerings
- How the respondent rates the school's buildings and grounds
- How the respondent rates the school's equipment (technology, science labs, etc.)
- How the respondent rates the school's services (counseling, transportation, etc.)
- How the respondent rates the faculty and staff of the school
- How the student is growing spiritually
- Whether the school is effectively growing Christian leaders
- Whether the respondent would recommend the school to a friend

Further, parents are asked questions regarding their expectations and actual experience. For example, each question allows them to indicate their initial expectation when joining the school or at the beginning of the school year. They are asked to respond again to the same question later, indicating their actual current experience. It is helpful to know the grade levels of the students and how long the family has attended the school. Such a survey could ask respondents to give a numerical rating for statements such as the following:

- My child is motivated to learn.

- The quality of instruction is high.
- There is good communication between school and home.
- The leadership and administration are effective.
- Class sizes are right.
- The school has caring, qualified Christian teachers.
- Support services are available (e.g., counseling, health care).
- The school promotes innovative educational experiences.
- I am able to volunteer and participate.
- There is a friendly community atmosphere.
- The education is biblical.
- My child will have an environment of Christian friends.

This information can help the board gain an understanding of the general condition and circumstances of the school.

FOR REFLECTION AND DISCUSSION

1. What are the present processes by which board members get accurate information about your school?

2. List some of the external measurement tools the school board could utilize to learn about school issues.

3. List some of the internal measurement tools the school board could utilize to learn about school issues.

4. What dashboard indicators would be useful for your board?

CHAPTER 19

Strategies to Advance the Mission

Once a school has put in the work of defining mission, has established curriculum and programs that are designed to accomplish the mission, and has measured the results so that school leaders know what the present status of the school is, it is time for the board to shoulder the task of advancing the mission.

Because of what is measured, the school leaders can assess the health and condition of various aspects of the school. The board can determine what areas seem to be strong and which areas are out of sync with the mission or appear to be weaker parts of the education process.

The board can then take action to correct the problems or take advantage of opportunities. Measurements have likely exposed items that call for immediate action. However, as the school gains a sense of balance, the better way to outline goals and priorities for improvement is by having a strategic plan.

SETTING THE DIRECTION AND PRIORITIES OF THE SCHOOL

The mission-directed governance model gives the school board the responsibility of determining the direction and priorities of the school. The board needs to know both where it is headed (the mission) and where it is at present (evaluation of current school programs and results based on measurement). Armed with accurate information, the board can sort through the vision ideas and form goals, objectives, plans, and priorities to reach the target. The board can further develop standards by which to measure progress and establish policies to guide the process.

The school head should very much be involved in the discussion with the board that analyzes the data and determines projects and priorities. The school head will likely be the primary person who suggests vision. But it is the school board's decision to determine the projects that have the highest priority.

ASSIGNING LEADERSHIP GOALS AND PROJECTS

How can the board maintain control of the conclusions reached regarding the school's direction and priorities? The board studies information from various sources as it determines the plans, steps, and priorities that will bring the school closer to its ideal. With this information the board can discuss and conclude what projects and priorities it will want to see accomplished. The board assigns three to six leadership goals and priorities as a mandate for the head of school to achieve in the next year. The number of assigned leadership projects may vary depending on the complexity of the issues.

The board may assign projects that require more than one year to accomplish. It is appropriate to consult with the school head on how much should be accomplished each year. Here are some examples of leadership projects that may include preparing a plan or accomplishing a plan or target:

- Prepare a plan that increases parking lot safety.
- Develop a plan that identifies and builds relationships with alumni.
- Prepare a school image survey that includes faculty, staff, parents, alumni, and high school students.
- Prepare a 15-year projection of student enrollment and of facility needs, including renovation and new construction. (Students entering preschool may have 14 or 15 years before graduating high school.)
- Initiate a program that encourages school volunteers and measures the number of volunteers and the hours they serve.
- Outline a plan for developing an integrated and comprehensive curriculum that conforms to the school's philosophy, goals, core curricular principles, and mission.

Having an agreed-upon mandate for leadership projects for the head of school is highly important. It allows the board to operate as a united team in determining what it wants to accomplish while avoiding debates concerning changes to priorities and the pursuit of new urgent directions proposed by individual board members. With such a plan the board can say no to other suggestions, considering them a diversion unless there is an emergency.

This brings greater unity among board members as well as between the board and the head of school. The head of school now has a better idea of his or her real priorities and can give full energy to accomplishing them. The resulting relationship between the board and the head of school is a partnership and a covenant that moves the school toward the mutually understood ideal. Mutual support, confidence, and trust grow as steps are taken that result in improvements as defined by the mission.

Ideally, these leadership projects should be an extension and implementation of the strategic plan of the school. It is best if the school leaders have a long-range plan of the school's direction, as this allows school leaders more balance in planning and anticipating budgetary and other support that may be necessary to achieve the desired results.

Before addressing a process for strategic planning, it is important to return to the subject of vision. The board needs to wrestle with vision possibilities and the actions the school should take to advance the mission. With the strategic plan the board will review these vision ideas and determine the actions that should be done to make the envisioned ideal more concrete.

VISION

What is the ideal? What should these aspects of education look like to more effectively raise Christian disciples who will advance Christ's kingdom? The school's vision statement should incorporate the philosophical mandate and the mission commitment and seek to develop ways to accomplish the mission in the current setting. It is composed of creative ideas that could help realize mission-based aspirations.

The school board must ensure that the vision consistently advances the mission. The mission will continue to be the overarching goal of the school over time. However, the vision will change because there will be changes in technology, environment, and education options. The school leaders will need to adjust their vision of how best to reach educational objectives within these challenges and opportunities.

It may be helpful to think of vision as a verb. Concepts such as "envisioning" or "brainstorming" come closest but still miss the intended nuance. Vision is not idle daydreaming, carefree mental wanderings, or flights of fantasy. Creating the vision is consciously using imagination to produce ideas to benefit and advance the mission. This should be an energetic, compelling, dynamic, and continuous exercise to purposefully seek more opportunities and more effective ways to cultivate whole-life disciples. Pursuing vision also means having the passion to explore improved ways of bringing students to Jesus Christ as Savior and Lord. Vision is the pursuit of imagining what ought to be.

The school's philosophy recognizes the Bible's mandate that sinners who are saved by the atonement of Christ are to become whole-life followers of

Christ and participate in a reformation by bringing all relationships under the authority of Christ. The mission states that the purpose of the Christian school is to help bring this about by training preschool-through-twelfth-grade students to become whole-life disciples who will change society and culture so that all of life advances Christ's kingdom. The vision prompts questions about what the school can do to more effectively cultivate such students; this calls for identifying the characteristics of the ideal student and then cultivating ideas of how to foster them. The mission-directed governance model promotes the mission, applies it to every area of the school by studied actions, and requires standards of measurement.

DISCUSSING VISION

One way to begin a school board discussion on vision is to allow each board member to spend a few minutes talking about what school was like when he or she was a child. What are the differences today? What circumstances could have been predicted? What changes have come as a surprise? What are the trends? What trends are likely to continue or expand? Are they opportunities or threats?

In addition to strengths, weaknesses, opportunities, and threats, the school should be asking questions such as these as the board considers strategic planning:

1. What really is the heart of the mission? What are the characteristics of the ideal student that the school should be nurturing?

2. What is the awareness and commitment of the board, administrative team, faculty, students, and school community to the school's mission and organizational structure?

3. What would be the characteristics of this school if it were focused entirely on producing such students?

4. What are the current ongoing projects and initiatives, and to what degree are they successfully advancing and promoting the mission?

5. What can the school do or offer to more effectively enhance its mission?

6. What steps can the school take to bring it closer to becoming a mission-directed Christian school?

7. How can the school ensure that initiatives will continue to be proposed that will advance the mission of the school and will not just identify current or past problems or individual preferences or agendas?

8. How does the school create a climate in which all participants seek to initiate proposals to produce better results?

9. How will initiatives be prioritized and governed to ensure that informed decisions are being made and that there is accountability?

10. What is changing in the social and cultural community, school community, families, churches, and competitive landscape?

11. What is changing in the field of education? How do those changes affect this school?

THE BOARD'S ROLE IN NURTURING AND MONITORING THE VISION

For strategic planning, the board of a Christian school needs to provide a vision that gives some sense of an ideal it aims to achieve.

The envisioning process usually is given leadership by the school head, often working with the faculty and staff. As the chief executive officer and the educational and organizational leader, the head of school represents all aspects of the school and brings together the educational expertise of the school personnel to pursue the ideal. The head of school works with the administrative team, department heads, teachers, and staff, and may have staff ad hoc committees working in concert to develop plans for school improvement. As a result of involving colleagues in this way, the head of school may propose to the board programs and policies that will bring the school closer to the ideal.

It also is natural for the board to ask for the head of school's recommendations for improvements as part of the various reports on the status of school programs. The board may require the head of school to prepare reports for the board concerning evaluation of present programs and how they contribute to producing the ideal student. The board may require the school head to prepare a plan of action to manage changes. As the board analyzes the information, it may agree on some needs and goals.

Additionally, in order to acquire a long-range perspective, the board may require a report on the head of school's perspective on the opportunities and possibilities reflected in the ad hoc committees' recommendations. The board could assign the head of school to report on possible new programs and services. The head-of-school reports should include a proposal, rationale, evidence, and recommendation of resources that will be needed to pursue the opportunities for improvement. The board then may use or revise these ideas to decide the direction and priorities of the school.

The board must create an environment that generates vision and also monitors and guides vision proposals. There can be thousands of ideas for improving student learning and school processes. The school needs to explore and sort these to determine which should be supported and which are distractions. Without conscious nurturing, vision ideas will die since there always are urgent pressures to handle immediate problems. Therefore, it is important for the board to monitor the development of vision in the following ways:

1. Encourage and insist on creating an environment that stimulates ideas that promote growth.

2. Discern and decide which vision ideas are to be pursued.

3. Turn vision ideas into goals and priorities.

4. Provide resources.

5. Provide accountability.

STRATEGIC PLANNING

The school's strategic plan identifies a target and the processes and priorities it will use to reach that target. A strategic plan usually refers to a broad-based holistic scheme that keeps the plan united and integrated while moving the whole school toward a broad educational target. Strategic plans usually anticipate that it will take the school several years to complete the process.

These discussions on strategic planning will consider two intertwined considerations. The first is student learning: For what kind of society and culture do students need to be prepared? What must the student learn, and what should the student become? The second consideration involves the school offerings: What must this school be like in order to prepare our students to have a personal relationship with Jesus as Savior and Lord and become fully equipped to advance Christ's kingdom?

A comprehensive strategic plan is often a bundle of single strands of plans. Because of the length of time it can take to carry out the comprehensive plan, school leaders often focus on one strand at a time. However, even when focusing on individual strands, it should be clear how each of these strands fits into the broader plan. For example, one strand of a school's strategic plan may include restructuring its financial practices. Another strand may be a long-range plan regarding facilities. Another strand may be a long-range plan for developing the curriculum. All of these strands are interdependent. For example, if the curriculum calls for purchase of new technology, this will have an impact on both facilities and finances. Strategic plans that are more comprehensive may take years or even decades to implement, while individual strands may be adjusted more quickly.

There are many formal programs to guide the process of constructing strategic plans for for-profit and nonprofit organizations. To guide the process, the board usually forms a suitably qualified ad hoc committee to act as the strategic planning team. The process likely begins with gathering information such as demographic statistics of the area, enrollment data, and various trends in school and community. The team needs to consider the trends of the community and speculate a little on where these could lead. The trends the team could discuss include changes in families, churches, religion and philosophy, government, education, economics, the influence of media and technology, and more. If these trends continue, what will the school be faced with? There are many sources for this information such as the chamber of commerce, city planning department, and real estate projections.

The strategic planning team typically involves many other people who discuss and analyze the school by considering the organization's strengths, weaknesses, opportunities, and threats (SWOTs). In the end, the team reports to the board on each characteristic and recommends actions that will correct the problems and enhance the strengths and opportunities. This report likely includes a recommendation for an action plan that addresses topics such as marketing, facilities, staffing, and finance.

Under mission-directed governance model, the school board ensures that the strategic plan is focused on the mission. Too often those who prepare strategic plans are institution-centered—concentrating on the viability of the organization by discussing how to gain more students, improve the school's financial situation, and have more impressive facilities. The problem with this sort of strategic plan is that it reduces what is important to what prospers the school as an institution, while ignoring why it is important for the school to exist at all. The board must ask what are the criteria used to determine whether a situation is a strength, weakness, opportunity, or threat. If the criteria considered are exclusively those that affect the organization's survival and prosperity instead of those that affect how the organization can more effectively accomplish the mission in the lives of the students, the strategic plan will not do all that it should do.

Institutional considerations are relevant and critical elements to consider, of course; however, under the mission-directed governance model the strategic planning process begins by focusing primarily on what will it take to properly educate the students. Institutional issues should be seen as means to accomplish this mission. The school leaders need to consider characteristics that preserve and advance the institution, but the leaders should focus on the institution's mission and the plan for nurturing the students to be trained as followers of Christ.

The mission-directed approach suggests that the organization follow SWOT or another systematic strategic planning process, but recommends that the process begin with one additional element—namely, the ideal. The strategic planning process should begin with the overall target of meeting the standards suggested in the mission statement. Among the first critical questions a strategic planning team should ask are, What are the characteristics of an ideal student? What would be the characteristics of this school if it were entirely focused on producing such students? How can the school more effectively enhance its mission? How can it move closer to becoming a Christian school with more evident fidelity to its mission? Only after considering these questions does it make sense to ask about what contribution the facilities, transportation, finances, lunch program, and so on make to cultivate this ideal student.

FOR REFLECTION AND DISCUSSION

1. Why should a school engage in strategic planning?

2. What do the school's ideals contribute to strategic planning?

3. How does having data from multiple sources become important for developing the strategic plan and goals for the next year?

4. How is your school's mission statement being used to generate ideals for programs and opportunities that will make the school more effective in reaching its mission in the coming years?

CHAPTER 20

Advancing the Mission Through the Budget

When in deep troubled waters, there is a significant difference between a person who is flailing so as not to drown and one who is attempting to swim to a destination. How can the board change its mindset from preventing failure to advancing the mission? The challenges of governance are probably most evident, intense, and concrete in producing the school budget. It seems Christian schools always live in the lean years.

Schools that don't have an effective mission often struggle with budgets. They often feel that they must reduce or at least prevent any significant increase in tuition, under the assumption that lower tuition will attract a greater number of students and generate more revenue.

The mission-directed governance model gives a few observations regarding school budgets.

1. There is constant pressure to keep tuition low and affordable for families. This is an admirable goal, but is seldom realistic. Costs for benefits such as insurance and pension regularly will increase above the rate of inflation. The budget will continue to expand to cover increased costs for buildings, maintenance, technology upgrades, and added educational services. Pressure to expand services comes from the requirement both to more effectively teach the school's philosophy and to meet the demands of families. If the school considers the teachers to be professionals and tries to give them a living salary, tuition will necessarily increase above the rate of inflation.

2. Having a unified strategic plan and agreement on leadership projects and priorities also means that the board must give the head of school adequate resources of time, money, and people to make the specified improvements. This has obvious consequences for balancing the budget and the amount charged for tuition. Preparing the new budget is more than adding an inflation percentage to last year's budget. It is at the budget level that the tuition and other revenues must balance with salaries and all expenditures, and resources for new goals must

also be provided. Because the board is united in its goals, it can determine the financial support needed to implement the long-range school plans and priorities, as well as what is needed to provide for contingencies of both opportunity and emergency.

3. It is important that the head of school propose the budget to the board. The head of school constructs the budget in conjunction with the business manager, administrators, department heads, athletic director, and others who have responsibility for revenue or expenditures, working with the whole school team to gather information to support educationally sound priorities. It is recommended that the head of school submit a draft budget to the board, with noted inclusions or reductions, a month before the formal budget proposal is presented. For example, these initial proposals might include an increased amount to initiate programs, hire new staff, and determine resources needed for the board-assigned leadership projects. These considerations can determine the goals for increases in salary and benefits as well as limits in tuition or other revenue. When a budget draft is proposed, the head of school can make a case for any necessary adjustments. This allows the finance committee and the board to be made aware of the proposed budget changes and the reasoning behind the proposals before the final budget decision is made. This also allows the board to identify and discuss the merits of the major proposals rather than justifying each line in the budget. If the expenditures are still too high, the board can give the school head a number that must be reached. The school head in turn can consult with other administrators and department heads to make cuts or recommend additional revenue options.

4. Especially in times when the school is doing better financially and the board is not requiring budget cuts, the board should prepare for the next financial downturn. (This is the strategy used by Joseph in Genesis 41.) It is wise to build into the budget a line item for future emergency expenditures. In addition, the school should ensure that there will be a positive cash balance at the end of the fiscal year. Assuming the school has a positive cash balance and a small amount for emergencies, these funds should be added to an investment account at the beginning of the new fiscal year. These funds accumulate in the good years, and they can be a lifesaver in the lean years. These funds should also provide funding for long-range maintenance projects such

as a new roof. This may allow the school to handle a major expenditure without a capital campaign.

BALANCING THE BUDGET IN HARD TIMES

In times of a struggling economy and reduced student enrollment, the school's choice of governance model does not eliminate the issues or spare the board from making difficult decisions. The board may be forced to cut some programs and restrict increases in employee salaries and benefits. The issue is whether the board is making the wisest decision based on all of the factors. However, under the mission-directed governance model the school addresses budget issues with an explicit focus on the school's mission.

The board wrestles with what cuts it should make. Boards try to maintain the status quo, but cannot. Typically boards try to make sure they are not cutting essentials, but they often conclude that it needs to trim "extras" such as music, art, and physical education. They must then freeze or cut employee salaries and benefits. Boards have cut long-range maintenance, postponed repainting the classrooms and decided they will use the outdated technology for one more year. Too often such reductions require an even larger increase in following years, so the cuts actually exacerbate the problems and create a greater crisis. The board's reduction of its offerings will finally result in striving for mere survival. This strategy does not work.

This is not to say that there should not be cuts or salarary freezes in crisis times. The premise of this chapter is that the board needs to talk about what is required to keep and advance the mission and purpose of the school and not make cuts impulsively. Mission-directed governance recommends that the budget approach include the following:

1. The board needs to discern the contribution of each line item to the mission. The board will often find it helpful to direct the school head to make budgetary recommendations. The head serves as chief educator and has a better sense of the purpose and contribution of each line item than a committee of noneducators who are also consumers. With a distinctive mission, it is possible for the boards to consider ideas that will advance the mission, provide distinctive whole-life Christian discipleship education, and attract families.

2. The school should constantly be considering multiple avenues to raising revenue. When board members consider each budget line item

as an expenditure only, there is little to do but figure out which ones to cut. Instead board members need to consider each line item as an investment that is meant to support the school's purpose. Board, administration, and faculty should be spending significant time considering opportunities that advance the school's mission and help the families and public understand the unique contribution their Christian school provides. This approach asks the board to spend as much time looking for investments and revenue enhancements as it does on cuts. Perhaps the expenses can be offset with a specific funding source. For example, aligning specific programs with specific goals allows the school to pursue grants from businesses, foundations, or families that may be willing to help fund an innovative idea. In addition, the board should explore alternate ways of funding general tuition or providing more tuition assistance. Many schools are enhancing their budgets by establishing foundations or thrift stores, signing contracts that permit cell towers on school property, or even starting for-profit businesses.

3. The board needs to acknowledge that it may have to make tough budget-cutting decisions. However, these tough decisions do not apply only to cuts. To be truly responsible, the board must also acknowledge that tough decisions may require keeping or even adding programs that distinguish the school, programs that should be considered an investment as they advance the school's mission, and programs that attract families.

COMMON STRATEGIES FOR KEEPING TUITION LOW

Of course the board must listen to calls for reviewing the budget to make it more efficient and to trim existing line items. But the board should realize that it has been trying to maintain a lean budget since the inception of the school. There is not likely a lot of "fat" in the budget to begin with. Most common strategies for keeping tuition low have undesirable consequences.

1. Here is a question for the board: Should keeping the tuition low be the board's top priority to attract and retain students?

   • Alas, the cost of tuition for Christian schooling will not likely match the low cost of the public school. But it is also important to note the reality that families don't select a school only on the basis of cost. While cost is a major factor, many families that are able to bear the cost are looking at the value of the education they are getting.

- If the school were to lose 10 percent of its students, would the loss come from those families making the greatest financial sacrifices, or from those who can most easily afford the tuition?

- To keep those who can least afford tuition, the school needs to look for ways to provide tuition assistance. To keep those who can best afford the education, the school must keep the quality and variety of educational offerings and the best and most qualified teachers.

- If the board cuts the attractive programs, it may be that the families who can afford the education are the ones who find another school. The result is that most of the families that remain at the school are the ones who can least afford the tuition. The board needs to keep the programs that families are convinced contribute to their children's growth in discipleship and open opportunities for their children's future.

- Remember, this same principle applies to retaining the best teachers. If the pay scale is too low, the best teachers might be tempted to leave, while the least experienced or those least likely to be hired elsewhere might stay. This affects the quality of education offered.

2. The determination not to raise tuition to pay for the cost of education can bring several consequences.

- Salaries or benefits are usually frozen or raises are minimal, with the result that employees bear a good portion of the sacrifice. Long-range maintenance suffers, advertising is reduced, and purchase of educational materials such as textbooks and classroom resources might be postponed. "Nonessential" or "elective" programs might be cut. All of these actions affect the quality of education provided by the school.

- The school likely will be forced to significantly raise revenue in the future to regain what is lost. For example, if textbooks are cut from the budget one year, the board needs to anticipate that at some point in the future, adding textbooks back into the budget will result in a very significant jump in tuition for one to three years.

3. A very common way for schools to add to revenue is to add fees for individual programs, combining a low tuition with payments for selected benefits.

- Some examples of such fees can include bus service, textbooks, participation in athletic programs, band and choir, and science and art classes.

- Experience shows that these additional fees frustrate and anger parents because the cost of tuition they anticipated is suddenly raised as a result of costs they did not anticipate or save for. To parents this looks like a disreputable bait-and-switch tactic.

4. One of the worst solutions is to simply require that all departments cut their operations by some specific percentage.

- This assumes that all programs have the same percentage of excess discretionary spending. Such an arbitrary reduction may weaken every program and make those already weak totally ineffective.

- Sometimes it is better to eliminate specific programs rather than to let them limp along on the edge of survival.

5. Boards often cut specific courses or programs.

- Since a very high percentage of the budget is related to employees, such cuts usually affect salaries and benefits.

- Employees are generally quite cooperative and willing to do their share. But the board needs to consider its own ethics of constantly requiring employees to bear the burden.

STRATEGIES FOR RAISING REVENUE

1. There are a number of ways to generate revenue. School leaders should recognize that the days of funding schools by relying almost exclusively on tuition are over. Schools should explore other revenue-generating approaches. Here are some approaches—besides tuition—that many schools use to generate funds:

- There is a myth that if the school could become larger by increasing the number of students, then the school will have financial stability. Increased enrollment will not rescue the school from its financial challenges. The reality is that an increase in the number of students enrolled will produce a bonanza only when the increase in tuition is greater than what was budgeted for expenditures that particular year. The reason that the windfall will last only one year is that the budget for the following year will anticipate the revenue from the current year's number of students. This increase in tuition revenue will likely produce an increase in associated expenditures; for example it may be necessary to hire an additional teacher and purchase extra textbooks, computers, and supplies. If student growth continues, at some point the school will need a part-time and eventually a full-time person to serve as an assistant administrator, athletic director, counselor, technology person, secretary, or other professional. The school may need to budget more for maintenance, and perhaps the school will eventually need additional classrooms. The reality is that student growth will not reduce the amount the school will charge for individual student tuition. The pattern is that an increase in tuition revenue will be offset by an increase in expenditures. The larger school may be able to afford some added services and may have a little more flexibility to handle financial emergencies, but large schools have most of the same budget problems as small schools.

- Some schools hold fund-raising events such as golf tournaments, art sales, and auctions.

- Schools may depend on funds generated by auxiliary associations that support various programs by hosting special events and projects.

- In many cases, local churches help support the school financially or help their parishioners with tuition assistance.

- Development departments can raise funds outside of tuition for special needs such as tuition assistance. Development departments may also raise money for capital projects such as constructing or renovating facilities, purchasing land, or providing transportation.

- Besides seeking immediate funds, there are long-range strategies to raise funds, such as encouraging people to remember the school in their will, to donate their business to the school upon their retirement, or to establish a personal insurance policy that will benefit the school. Another long-range strategy is to establish a foundation to secure funds for an endowment.

2. There are other less-common strategies for generating revenue.

- Occasionally grants are available from businesses or foundations, generally for specific projects outside of the general budget. These are usually one-time opportunities and usually for projects that are new programs, rarely for continued support.

- It is sometimes possible to generate funds from renting the property or by contracting to have cell towers or commercial advertising signs installed.

- The school can explore establishing nonprofit business enterprises that will support the school. Thrift stores or other enterprises support some schools.

- Schools should seriously consider establishing for-profit business enterprises that can feed a percentage of profits back to the school. This can be done legally with a for-profit business existing separately and paying taxes, but having its board selected by the Christian school board. These opportunities can be used for student learning as well. Examples of businesses that could be considered are a car wash, a beauty parlor that rents space to beauticians, a small restaurant, a storage facility, or a coffee business.

3. There are opportunities to increase school offerings to creatively and visibly expand the mission. In light of its defined mission and its identified purpose and focus, the school may be forced to make some cuts, but it also can be open to ways of making its education more deliberate and to purposefully expand school programs. Here ae just a few of the programs that schools have successfully provided:

- Offering online courses

- Offering college dual-enrollment courses

- Developing a specialized student curriculum to develop leadership skills and experiences

- Developing personalized education to partner with home instruction

- Developing a specialized business enterprise curriculum with students

- Partnering with churches for a mentoring program

- Having an on-campus international student program

- Offering summer camp programs and tutoring services

- Affiliating with Christian schools in other countries

- Establishing learning through technology, such as with a student tablet or laptop program

- Developing a written service curriculum and offering extensive service opportunities such as tutoring students at a local public elementary school or tending a community garden

4. Many of these programs don't really cost much, and some may generate income, but they do contribute to nurturing whole-life Christian disciples who are already engaged in bringing all relationships and culture under the authority of Jesus Christ. When the board focuses on the mission of the school, this does help develop criteria for making tough decisions. These experiences are visible to the parents and the community and show the school's commitment and creative approach to Christian education.

5. In order to sustain willingness to invest financial resources, it is critically important that the whole school community be able to explain what is unique about the ministry of the school, and they all need to be convinced that the school is achieving that goal.

FOR REFLECTION AND DISCUSSION

1. What is the process your school follows to form its budget?

2. Does the school budget provide funding for the elements needed to advance the mission of the school? Please discuss and provide examples.

3. What opportunities exist that could generate more income?

CHAPTER 21

Head-of-School Reports

How will the board actually determine the direction the school should take? The board needs accurate information about the present situation of the school. How can the board be assured that it is getting all the information it needs and that the information is accurate? While many aspects of the school are being measured, how will the board be informed about the results? It is important that the board have truthful, reliable, and complete information so that it can pilot the school on a steady course in this changing world.

The primary sources of information available to the board are reports from the head of school. There are four important types of report that the school head should present to the school board.

1. GENERAL INFORMATION REPORTS

In most schools, this is the typical report the school head submits each month. This report gives information to the board on present events and issues, along with anecdotal success stories of a student or teacher who received some special recognition. It may contain material about a faculty workshop, grandparents day, or band concert. It should contain a list of coming events on the school calendar so that board members may attend or at least be able to talk intelligently about them.

2. PROGRAM EVALUATION REPORTS

The board does have a responsibility to assure the owner that all parts of the school are contributing to the mission. The board will want to be assured that the school offerings and programs are directed toward effectively accomplishing the school's mission. The school head is responsible for all school programs, and so should be responsible for reporting to the board regarding the present health, success, and value of school programs.

The mission-directed governance model uses a technique that provides the board with all the relevant information. The board designates the school head to present a written evaluation of a specified program. A format for the program evaluation could be as follows:

- Statement of the program and the reason why this program evaluation is being presented

- Relevant current board policies that govern this program area

- Description and history of the program with relevant data, purposes of the program, and how it is meant to contribute to achieving the school's mission.

- Evaluation of the program with strengths and weaknesses

- School head recommendations for the program and whether the board should add or change board policies related to the program

There can be many motivations for the board to ask for a program evaluation, including dissatisfaction. Without raising the issue before the whole board, an individual board member with a question may communicate directly with the school head at any time and can probably get a quick answer to the question. However, sometimes the answers are complex, and it may be necessary to probe a bit deeper. In such cases, the question can be presented to the board through the usual channels to get it added to the board agenda. After discussion, the whole board may ask for a program evaluation. (Note: A request for a formal report should come only as an action by the whole board, not as an independent assignment from an individual board member.)

Here is an example of this process in action. The board of a Christian school had some significant questions about the school's athletic program. Are the athletic teams producing athletes that display the attitudes and behaviors associated with professional sports rather than those associated with a Christian outlook?

In such a situation the head of school may prepare a report summarizing the athletic program, including survey results along with observations and advice from the appropriate staff people. The head of school's written report can provide general information to help the board understand the issues. The report evaluating a specific program may include the history and context of the program, present board policies, and issues for attention. The report may include the philosophy and goals of athletics in the school, athletic offerings at the various grade levels, facilities for athletics, level of competition, quality and background of coaches, and any special concerns that may have been suggested. The report may include the process of hiring coaches and their requirements, training of the coaches in the school's mission, and expectations of coaches in their relationships with athletes and their families. It may identify additional administrative policies or other materials designed to carry out the board's policies, and perhaps even the head of school's recommendation for new board policies. The written report should be distributed to all board members several days before the board meeting so that they can read it in preparation for the meeting.

At the time of the report to the board, the athletic director, principal, and others who may be directly involved in preparing the report or who contribute directly to the athletic program may be present at the board meeting to offer their perspectives on the issues and to answer questions. The board president, head of school, or athletic director likely will have some introductory or summary comments. The board will review the report and then ask questions or make comments.

Rather than asking for reports that come only from dissatisfaction, it is worthwhile for the board to schedule reports from the school head on various school departments such as maintenance, transportation, the business office, and food service. It is exhilarating for the board to hear employees explain their role in contributing to the cause of Christian education. It also is a tremendous encouragement for these employees to know that the board recognizes the importance of their role.

For example, the board may ask the head of school to report on school programs that help students with learning differences or difficulties. The head of school likely would involve teachers from special education, special reading programs, math enhancement programs, study skills development, or similar programs. The report may address the longevity of the programs, the number of students and teachers involved, a case for the programs, school costs, special sources of revenue, and statistics showing statistical improvement in test scores, socialization, retention, graduation, and vision for the future. The report likely would include a vision of what the programs need in order to become more successful. With some of the program specialists present, there can be good question-and-answer sessions to cover what is known and what needs to be investigated in the future.

Board members are usually delighted that they can learn about a topic just because it is interesting and provides them with examples of excellent programs to talk about with their friends. The board may look for an in-depth understanding of topics that don't normally come to the board's attention. The head of school may suggest reports that would be helpful to indicate an area needing the board's attention or an area in which the school is proud of its unique success. Through head-of-school reports the board is much more informed on subjects such as service-learning, curricular mapping, the number and types of extracurricular activities offered at the various grade levels, the number and types of field trips and other educational experiences, how textbooks are selected, how teacher evaluations are conducted, professional development, the international student program, student counseling, technology, financial procedures, employee insurance, pensions and other benefits, employee job descriptions, and many more matters.

A school board may schedule specific opportunities for individual board members to suggest topics for head-of-school reports. The executive committee considers this list with the head of school to determine a schedule. If there are too many suggestions, the executive committee recommends which topics to postpone. The list and schedule are brought to the board at the next meeting, with the option that the board can change the executive committee's recommendation. In this way, the board as a whole determines which reports it should receive and which should have priority. This again allows the board to act as a whole unit. It is a way to ensure that the most significant issues come before the whole board.

Program evaluation reports on specific areas have proven to be one of the most interesting and meaningful ways for the board to have oversight of the school. These reports not only have helped the board identify problem areas, but they also have enabled the board to regularly learn of successes.

After the associates involved with the presentation are dismissed, the board may discuss the program evaluation report further. The board may have a variety of responses to a program evaluation report:

1. The board may accept the report for information with no board action since the board is satisfied that board policies are being carried out.

2. The board could give a mandate to the head of school to meet specified goals in the annual leadership projects and priorities or for some other specified time period. Leadership projects will be discussed later in this chapter.

3. The board could ask that the school head submit a follow-up report to give further information or an action plan. For example, the school (referred to above) in which the board had concerns about the character of athletics required the school head to submit a further study and also a plan of action to bring the school's athletic programs more in alignment with the school's mission. The plan was developed with input

from coaches, players, and parents. The school found it could still have winning teams, but now with a better Christian testimony that affected not only their school, but also the league in which they play.

4. The board may form an ad hoc committee with a stated mandate, such as whether this is an appropriate area for a head-of-school leadership project or whether the board needs to clarify the expectations by adding or revising board policies. The ad hoc committee could study the concerns along with the head of school and prepare a written response to the board mandate to be presented at a designated board meeting.

It should be noted that the board oversees programs, not people. The only person the board evaluates is the head of school. It is the head of school's job to hire, evaluate, and (if necessary) fire other school employees. The board evaluates people or their job performance only through the head of school. This is a most effective way to ensure accountability for job performance. All decisions of the head of school are subject to appeal to the board.

3. MEASUREMENT REPORT

As discussed in a previous chapter, the board decides by policy what it expects to measure. The board requires the school head to submit measurement reports at designated board meetings. The board will insist on measurement of academic progress, student understanding of the core curricular principles, and various strands purposefully included in the curriculum such as service-learning, student discipleship, and student leadership. The school head will also write measurement on the effect of extracurricular offerings, clubs, and organizations.

The board will also insist that there be measurements of how effective school programs are in accomplishing the intended results. The board will want to know about the school and its composition—information on the number and quality of teachers, its finances, and so on.

The school head is required to present the appropriate data and information in a single comprehensive report. This allows the whole board to have all of the relevant data. This will provide the information needed for determining the steps for advancement and strategic planning. We will see how this report also gives figures that will become part of the evaluation of the school as a whole, and also of the school head.

4. LEADERSHIP PROJECTS REPORTS

Leadership project reports are about projects the board has assigned to the school head. They inform the board of progress and assure the board that the project will be completed at the designated time.

SCHEDULING REPORTS

In the board calendar, both the school measurement report and the leadership projects reports often fit best at the November meeting.

Obviously this is a decision for each school, but assuming the board meets monthly, the school head may be able to submit approximately eight program evaluation reports per year.

How can the board be assured that these reports are accurate and don't give just the positive side? First, there is the integrity of the head of school. Second, there is no advantage in giving a false report since the difficulties will soon appear. Third, the head of school's report usually is written with the help of many other school people, so the head could not get away with writing a false report. Fourth, the board's contact with other information, both formal and through contacts with others associated with the school, will reveal any inconsistencies. Fifth, there is opportunity for question and answer, so the board will know how much time and effort went into preparing the report and what reference points were used.

Confident that it has reliable, accurate, and complete information, the board can move from concentrating on protecting the school to focusing its attention on ways to promote and advance the school's mission.

FOR REFLECTION AND DISCUSSION

1. Why is it helpful to have the head of school prepare a report on the topic to be discussed?

2. Describe each of the four reports the school head is expected to submit to the school board. How does each of these reports help the school board in its governance?

3. List a few topics on which it would be helpful for your head of school to make a program evaluation report.

4. What top three leadership projects would you consider appropriate to give to your head of school for the next year?

CHAPTER 22

Evaluating the Head of School

in other books on governance, the topic of head-of-school evaluation may be discussed in conjunction with the head of school's role. The reason for placing it here is to avoid the trap of reducing the head of school's role to managing the categories found in the typical job description. Therefore, the decision was to first cover the mission of the school, advancement of the mission, nonnegotiables, school measurement, head-of-school reports, and board-assigned leadership projects. To understand head-of-school evaluation, it is necessary to understand the board's role and the tools the board uses to assign projects and priorities to advance the school toward its mission. The head of school is accountable to the board for the results of these assignments, even if the head of school delegates the assignment to others.

This chapter will discuss the controls available to the board to guide and limit the head of school. The board will write policies that govern the head of school's process of decision making, and the board will prevent problems through head-of-school evaluation.

THE BOARD EVALUATES THE HEAD OF SCHOOL

The mission-directed governance model emphasizes some unique aspects of head-of-school evaluation. For example, while a minimum expectation may be that the school is well managed, the head of school's evaluation should be focused on how effectively the head of school advances the school's mission.

The board's evaluation must be based on the degree to which the head of school is accomplishing the board directives. The mission-directed model emphasizes that there is to be improvement in the school, not just maintenance of the status quo. As we have seen, a report on the measurement results determined by board policy, assigned special leadership projects, and written reports from the head of school are all tools available to the board. The head of school's evaluation must be the result of board deliberation, not a tally of the opinions of those accountable to the head of school.

The board may find it helpful on occasion to be aware of others' opinions on various aspects of the school, as long as observation and evaluation are distinguished. Observation is recognizing that someone may have an opinion on the head of school's performance. An evaluation is a conclusion on the part of the board; the evaluation usually includes both a list of commendations and areas identified for improvement.

One area the board might evaluate is whether the head of school treats people with Christian principles—fairly, consistently, and with respect. The board may poll employees, parents, and others for evidence of these attributes, data which can contribute to the board's evaluation. While the head of school's evaluation may include observations of faculty understanding and support, these should not constitute the evaluation.

If the board does solicit staff observations, some teachers could complete a survey without having experience or a broadly informed opinion; they may be merely circling a number to complete the survey. Having the employee write sentences in response to questions instead of circling "excellent" to "poor" can elicit more helpful information.

The mission-directed model insists that all observers sign their observation forms. This allows the board member to follow up on individual employee responses, especially if an employee has accused the head of school of malfeasance or raised other potential legal or ethical issues. However, respondents need assurance that individual responses are known only by the board-designated recipient and never by the head of school.

The results of board evaluation emphasize the unity in direction and priority that exists between the board and the school head. The mission-directed governance model gives the head of school the opportunity to explain how the challenges established by the board were met and exceeded. The head of school should be directly accountable to the board, and both the board and the head of school should know the issues and criteria that are the basis of the evaluation.

Under the mission-directed model, the head of school is under the protection of the board. If the head of school is attacked by staff or constituents for taking certain actions in carrying out board policies, he or she can seek confirmation and encouragement from the board. Evaluations are based on whether the head of school has accomplished predetermined, understood job-performance expectations. This gives the board an opportunity to praise and encourage the head of school on the basis of measured improvement.

WHAT IF THERE ARE AREAS OF CONCERN?

Since the head of school is human, there will be times when the board has concerns and will look for improvement. What does the board do if it concludes the head of school deserves a mixed review, with areas that need improvement? The process of evaluation will raise issues that are a concern of the board as a whole. These issues can be shortcomings in managing people and projects, completing board assignments, or following board policies. These issues may include any aspect of management, such as enforcement of discipline, having too many typographical errors in the school newsletter, or lack of employee supervision.

One option is to require the head of school to submit a report to the board or board executive committee on an issue of concern. If there is time, this approach will notify the head of school of the concern and provide the opportunity to give background information to help the board understand complex issues. The board could include an identified concern as one of goals that the head of school is to accomplish during the next school year. If the issue is more urgent, the board may determine a more aggressive timeline for improvement. Normally such close monitoring would take place with the supervision of the executive committee or a board ad hoc committee, with designated milestones for the head of school to give evidence of progress.

Inadequate improvement ultimately may lead to the dismissal of the head of school. The process for correcting or dismissing the head of school should be stated in board policies. The final decision to dismiss the head of school should be made by the whole board.

If the evaluation shows that the board lacks confidence in the person, the board must determine whether this is due to the person's inexperience or personal characteristics. If experience is the issue, the board can support the head of school with training, or perhaps mentoring by a more experienced school head from another school. If the board's concern is with personal characteristics of the school head, the board may create an improvement program with established times and criteria for assessing progress. While the mission-directed governance model can't solve people problems or suddenly change personal characteristics, it can provide an environment in which people can grow into the role of head of school.

BOARD POLICIES FOR POOR ACTIONS BY THE HEAD OF SCHOOL

In an earlier chapter we considered how board policies guide and limit the head of school's administrative decisions. However, board members may fear that if they are not making or approving each decision, an incompetent or aggressive school head may cause trouble. For example, one day a board member of a school with a serious financial problem drove by some acreage owned by the school and noticed a for-sale sign on it. The school head had decided the best strategy to meet the financial crisis was to sell a piece of school property without the knowledge or permission of the board. How can the school prevent such situations?

The board establishes written policies that provide criteria that the head of school of school must use in decision making. For example, these policies require decisions to be legal, ethical, and in compliance with standard financial or other practices. The board also establishes policies that limit the head of school's authority, including limits on the sale of real estate or other property above a specified amount, or on incurring school debt. The board should consider other policies that prevent the head of school from changing his or her own salary or benefits, signing contracts above a specified amount or over a designated number of years, or spending money other than what was approved in the general operating budget or other accounts approved by the board.

Another way to prevent surprises or crises is to have the head of school periodically report to the board on issues being considered or explored, perhaps following each group of topics in the board policy handbook. This allows board members to discuss the issues and respond with encouragements or cautions.

If the head of school takes action contrary to an established board policy, the board needs to know what it can do if a serious problem arises. In a crisis situation, board action need not wait until the regularly designated evaluation time. Such urgent situations may include the head of school being accused of a crime, a brazen misuse of authority, an immoral action, or a flagrantly subversive attitude or action against the board. Dismissing a head of school for malfeasance or a personal ethical or moral lapse should be covered by policy. In a critical situation, the board president may place the crisis on the board agenda at a regular or special meeting. Policies should dictate the process (for example, a policy could be written to allow the board to meet in executive session without the head of school). The policies should include the process whereby the head of school may respond before the issue becomes public.

EBB AND FLOW

Because governing, managing, and leading are done by and for people, there is an ebb and flow in the relationship between the board and the head of school. The level of confidence and experience influences how interested the board is in the details of what the head of school is doing and the sensed need for new written policy.

The ideal is for both the board and the head of school to be committed, strong, far-thinking, organized communicators. If both are strong, the mission-directed governance model will provide an excellent tool to define their roles and the processes for decision making, reducing potential competition between the two. The worst situation is for both the board and the head of school to be weak, passive, or prone to politics.

The mission-directed governance model can bring out the best in the head of school and board. If the board is inexperienced but has confidence in a strong school head, it can expect to lean on the head of school for leadership and vision within the context of policies, training, and commitment to a common vision.

TIMELINE FOR EVALUATION OF THE SCHOOL HEAD

The following is a suggestion for a fruitful process and timeline for evaluating the head of school:

1. The board and head of school discuss in January (and normally conclude in February) a number of leadership goals and priority projects. The board also creates a list and schedule of reports required from the head of school.

2. The head of school submits the requested reports as designated throughout the school year.

3. In October the board decides whether observations regarding the head of school are to be solicited from the faculty or other constituents.

4. At the November board meeting the head of school submits a written report on the progress made on each of the leadership goals and priorities, noting when associated reports were submitted.

5. At this time the head of school also submits documentation of improvements in the school during the school year.

6. Solicitation of observations from faculty, staff, parents, or other constituents, if desired, occurs in November. These are given to the board president, who shares the results with the executive committee.

7. In December, board members submit their individual observations and comments to the executive committee.

8. Also in December, the executive committee gathers observations and information and prepares a draft of the evaluation and a recommendation to the board regarding the head of school's contract.

9. The board president meets with the head of school to discuss the executive committee's conclusions. The head of school may request to meet with the executive committee to explain or discuss aspects of the report. The executive committee may or may not revise the evaluation report that it submits to the full board at its next meeting.

10. In January, the board meets for a period of time in executive session, without the head of school present, to discuss the evaluation of the head of school. The board decides whether a contract is to be offered for the next school year and whether conditions, commendations, or timelines are to be attached. The board and head of school meet to conclude the evaluation and begin the process of identifying what new leadership projects and priorities and head-of-school reports to the board should be assigned.

SAMPLE SURVEY QUESTIONS

The following are suggestions for the type of questions included in a survey of the faculty and staff or other school constituents regarding the performance of the head of school. Each respondent is expected to sign his or her name, although it must be made clear that the school head will not know who signed the observation form. The name is requested so that the board can ask follow-up questions to respondents who raise serious concerns.

1. How effectively does this person articulate the philosophy of the school, both in writing or speaking?

2. How effective is the head of school in representing the school's mission and programs to the broader community?

3. How would you characterize the head of school's effectiveness in providing vision, developing short-range and long-range goals, and practicing management skills that accomplish that vision?

4. How effective is the head of school's spiritual leadership?

5. How effective in the head of school's performance in leading people, building teams, and maintaining morale?

6. How effective are the head of school's professional and personal attributes, including decision making, fairness, availability, communication, and so on?

7. What specific areas do you want to point out as strengths of the head of school?

8. What specific recommendations would you identify for improvement?

9. Do you have additional comments?

FOR REFLECTION AND DISCUSSION

1. What is the difference between an observation and an evaluation?

2. Why is it the school board's responsibility to evaluate the head of school?

3. On what types of issues should the board seek observations from staff or parents?

4. Why should the evaluation of the head of school be linked to the evaluation of the school?

5. What can the board do if the head of school is out of compliance with board policies?

PART FOUR

Reflections, Decisions, and Directions

CHAPTER 23

Board Responsibilities and Tools of Direction and Control

The board has a variety of effective tools available for governing the school and being accountable to the owner. This chapter summarizes the responsibilities of the board and its tools of direction and control under the mission-directed governance model.

1. Determine the organization's philosophy, purpose, and mission.

- The owner and the board determine the ideal toward which the school community strives. The essential definitions of mission and purpose are written in the school's covenant.

- The board establishes policies to identify the nonnegotiables to be protected and preserved, as well as policies that identify the mission and vision the school is to promote.

2. Be accountable to the owner for protecting the nonnegotiables, ensuring consistent philosophical direction and operations of the school, and promoting and advancing the mission and the vision of the school.

- The board reports to the owner its conformity to the philosophy and mission of the school.

- The board needs approval from the owner to amend the covenant.

- The owner authorizes the board to take any action that would be an exception to the covenant.

- The board recommends to the owner a list of eligible board candidates for election by the owner.

3. Determine the school's governance model.

- The board determines whether the school will follow the traditional model, the governance-by-policy model, or the mission-directed governance model.

- The board establishes policies regarding governance operations and limits.

4. Determine the characteristics essential to the curriculum.

- The board establishes the core curricular principles and policies to ensure that the school's essential founding principles are taught to the students.
- The board requires testing of student performance on the core curricular principles.

5. Determine the criteria for the daily management practices and operations of the school.

- The board establishes policies to meet the criteria and principles that guide the management and decisions of the administration.
- The board as a whole must vote to initiate new policies or amend existing policies.
- The board as a whole must vote to authorize any exception to an existing board policy.

6. Determine the vision, goals, direction, and priorities of the school.

- The board initiates action by establishing the target and by mandating the leadership goals and priorities for the head of school.
- The board controls action by defining policy that lists the specific decisions the board will make. These specific decisions may include the following:

  a. Approval of the budget

  b. Approval of major fund-raising efforts

  c. Approval of major capital projects

  d. Sale or purchase of property

  e. All recommendations to the owner, including amendments to the covenant and qualified candidates for the board

  f. Consideration of new policies or amendments to present policies

  g. Appeals from individuals or groups on decisions made by school personnel

    h. Establishing goals and priorities

    i.   Determining policies that define criteria of school programs

    j.   Evaluating the head of school and holding him or her accountable

7. Evaluate every program and aspect of the school to ensure that it is meeting needs, is bringing the school closer to the ideal, is reflecting organizational planning, and is well managed.

- The board establishes the criteria by which it will evaluate the school as a whole.
- The board requires the head of school to submit reports evaluating designated school programs.
- The board has the authority to collect observations—through means such as surveys and polls—from those who are part of the school.
- The board has the authority to solicit observations from those outside the school when it requests reports on specific areas (e.g., conclusions made by accrediting organizations, accounting firms reporting on a financial review, and reports from health code or fire code enforcers).
- The board has the authority to establish ad hoc committees to review areas in which policy additions or changes may be necessary.

8. Ensure that auxiliary organizations are partners of the school and are supportive of the school's directions and priorities.

- The board recognizes each auxiliary organization.
- The board establishes policies that ensure that auxiliary organizations enhance the school within the guidelines determined by the board.

9. Govern itself as a whole unit, striving for a common goal.

- The board establishes policies that allow members of the school community to strive toward a common goal.
- The board as a whole may hear appeals.
- The board recruits new board members.
- The board assesses its own performance.
- The board establishes the leadership priorities to be completed by the head of school.

- The board as a whole makes specific decisions, including setting its annual agenda.

- The board promotes and enhances the school's vision and image.

- The board personally and publicly supports new ideas and programs as well as seeks to promote contact with organizations or persons that may help support the school.

10. Hold the head of school accountable to manage the school in a way that is consistent with the mission and board policies.

- The board hires the head of school.

- The board supports the head of school and assesses the head of school's performance.

- The board designates the leadership goals and priorities to be accomplished by the head of school.

- The board awards or withholds the head of school's contract, with incentives or conditions.

The board has the tools to control every aspect of the school by policies and specified decisions. This includes the school's nonnegotiables, school operations, and holding the head of school accountable for all areas of the school. The board determines the school's direction and priorities, and it evaluates the head of school not only on management skills but also on how well he or she contributes to achieving the board's mandates to reach the mission.

FOR REFLECTION AND DISCUSSION

1. Review each of the summarized responsibilities of the board and describe how a board controls the direction of the school. How does your school exemplify these descriptions?

2. How is your school board empowered so that each member can serve as a trustee for the whole school community?

CHAPTER 24

Making the Change

It is critically important that the leaders who advocate a change of governance model be aware of the energy and commitment it will take to introduce the changes—and that they follow the decision through to completion. Such a fundamental change will not be easy or without opposition. Some people will say "I told you so" when loss of momentum, new problems, or other complaints appear. Perhaps change in a ministry such as a Christian school is especially difficult because no one wants to make a mistake with the education of children.

Almost any change will bring resistance, and resistance may come from deep, unarticulated reasons rather than from stated concerns. Some hesitate because change necessarily means some unpredictability. Familiarity with the present arrangement offers security, and it may be easier to keep making familiar mistakes with known costs than to put a lot of energy into a new endeavor with an unknown price. People who are tentative will call for vigilance, caution, and slow change.

Doubts and questions will arise. Doubters may maintain that the school shouldn't implement any change until the last doubt has been eliminated and there is complete consensus. They may suggest that this is not the right time or may argue that such a model will work only in a bigger or smaller school. They may appeal to tradition or point out that the old model of governance has worked for many years and the new one may be a fad. Such questions are legitimate but sometimes can be a strategy to make the proposal disappear. No one wants to be branded as part of the group that made a blunder with the precious ministry. It is safer to let the next board, or generation, take such risks—or wait for a crisis to force change.

Some approach a change in governance models as a win/lose situation, expecting that those who advocate the present model must make the most concessions. True, the mission-directed governance model does intentionally challenge the status quo; it seeks to establish a different order of power and authority. Each part of a school constituency is familiar with its present territory and domain of influence. Constituents know how the present model works and how to get the results they seek. Under a new model, they may lose influence or visibility and will have to jockey for a new position or learn a new strategy of influence. This does not mean to imply that all such concerns are selfish and merely power politics; all parties love the school and want what is in its best interests. Each group wants to ensure it will retain at least the same voice and influence, and fears the consequences if the new model doesn't work out.

Those in the leadership group who intend to bring change must be convinced of its necessity and must often remind themselves of that fact. The issue is not only the present condition of the school but the wider trends that give a strong rationale for changing the school now, rather than waiting for a crisis of survival. The leadership group must communicate to the broader school constituency the consequences of trying to maintain the same course in light of these encroaching trends. The questions for the board and the leadership of the school are whether such a change is the best thing for the school, whether this is the right time, and whether conditions might allow an easier transition later.

Rather than let these issues surface as a surprise, we can take an educated guess as to what some of the questions and challenges from various school groups will be. Here are some of those issues, along with responses.

OBJECTIONS FROM THE OWNER

1. For many parochial or church-owned schools under a traditional model, church leaders were able to delve into any area of the school at any time and make changes. They could act without standard procedures and without recourse. This same situation may exist when a particular individual owns the school.

   Response: This authoritarian approach can fracture relationships and lead to stagnation. Overbearing ways cause hard feelings; perhaps Ephesians 6:4 ("Fathers, do not exasperate your children") applies here. In such a setting, the board takes a mostly passive role—timidly seeking to be safe, trying to avoid mistakes, making no waves—rather than exerting its energy and attention to advance the mission. For a good relationship between the church and the board, the governance model should establish clearly identified roles, authority, limits, and processes.

2. Under ownership by an independent association, the members of the association may be reluctant to change. Those with close connections to board members might feel the loss of direct influence over specific areas of the school. Those with complaints may be uncomfortable with new processes for addressing grievances. Some parents may view the school as "parent run" and believe that parents should be able to make enough noise to change circumstances for their children. Many may be unhappy with the change in their social position and influence. Parents also may feel disenfranchised because they are no longer invited to serve on standing committees or directly participate in school operations. They may wonder whether the board is, in fact, in control, and question whether the head of school or others have too much power.

    Response: The board needs to proactively communicate what is being done and the reasons why it is considering changes. Only if the board is empowered with governance can it concentrate on advancing the mission rather than simply responding to individual problems. Communication should assure the community that the board now will have more knowledge and control of school operations and the ability to measure achievement and hold people accountable. The board must explain the process for participating in school issues as well as for resolution of complaints. These policies and processes will bring better results. The new model protects what is most valuable to the constituency and permits thoughtful decisions and creative advancement of the school's mission.

OBJECTIONS FROM THE BOARD

1. While the mission-directed governance model empowers the board as a whole, it also reduces the role of individual board members. Some board members may lament not being the first line of contact for problems from faculty or parents. They may feel weak or without influence if they can't immediately and personally resolve complaints.

    Response: It is important to emphasize that the mission-directed governance model provides processes to find the best solutions for problems. The mission-directed model works for board consensus, makes issues more predictable, and calls all board members to serve as trustees of the whole school rather than as representatives of particular groups. By operating within the designated process to solve problems, the board as a whole will gain credibility and the confidence of faculty and constituents.

2. Under the mission-directed model, board meetings can become routine, lasting only a couple of hours. Some may miss the drama and thrill of finger-pointing or emotional argument.

   Response: This is precisely one of the blessings that a school hopes to experience—to operate as a unified team advancing the mission. Discussion and debate centers on topics such as the need to establish or modify board policies, proposals for standards of measurement, and goals for the head of school's leadership projects. The board will continue to discuss the budget, tuition, and similar issues. Board discussion usually is centered on head-of-school reports. Much of the board's task is to learn about and monitor educational programs and opportunities, and discussion may center on information rather than on strong opposing views. The board has more information at its disposal and a better sense of balance concerning whether an issue is actually urgent.

3. School boards under the governance-by-policy model are able to make decisions efficiently. However, it is possible that some board members feel disconnected from the day-to-day life of the school.

   Response: The mission-directed governance model utilizes the best of both the traditional model and the governance-by-policy model. It uses the effective decision-making process found in the governance-by-policy model. It also establishes processes intended to prevent the board from drifting away from the school's mission, philosophy, and nonnegotiables. A clear covenant with the school's owner, a head of school who supports and promotes the school's mission, and mission-directed board policies keep the board on track. The head of school continually interacts with the board through scheduled reports to the board and implementation of board policies. The board is thus directed and empowered to lead the school toward an agreed-upon mission.

4. Under the mission-directed model, the board is required to develop a comprehensive vision and proactive direction for the school—which

may not have been a significant part of its activity. People may think this will take too much work.

> Response: Developing a comprehensive and proactive direction is precisely what motivates many people to serve on the board. The board cannot simply wait for issues to come to the board for resolution. The proactive vision is disseminated to all of the departments of the school so that everyone understands the school's direction and priorities. The board, the administration, the faculty, and all members of the school community are committed to implement the vision with acknowledged accountability to Jesus Christ for every aspect of the school.

OBJECTIONS FROM FACULTY AND STAFF

1. Some faculty members who have enjoyed special influence with or access to individual board members under the traditional model may feel threatened by the mission-directed governance model. Under this model, faculty members will not have representatives to whom to express opinions, nor will they vote directly on issues such as budget, facilities, or educational matters that were the task of standing committees. Instead, the head of school represents faculty interests before the board. This loss of control is of primary concern to long-term faculty who have had such influence in the past.

   > Response: Under the traditional model, teachers could only express their opinions through a few influential teacher representatives. Most teachers did not participate in discussing key topics or have direct access to the decision makers. The mission-directed model gives faculty and staff more direct participation. The faculty contributes, under the authority of the head of school, by serving on department committees, peer team meetings, and ad hoc committees regarding various curricular and operational issues. Workshops, brainstorming sessions, and ad hoc committees about student learning, curriculum, educational experiences, and broad school issues all encourage faculty to express opinions, propose changes, and express their thoughts about the operations of the school; they are not limited to considering only identified school problems. The head of school interacts with the board regarding faculty issues.

2. Some faculty may be concerned about curricular mapping and integration of core principles into the curriculum. Teachers may feel offended if they think the curricular changes being made are a signal that they are unappreciated or that they weren't doing an adequate job in the classroom before.

> Response: Under the mission-directed governance model, the articulation of curriculum is required precisely because teachers are so valuable. Curricular mapping can help teachers new to the school understand the school goals and expectations in curriculum and how what was taught in the grade before and what will be taught in the next grade fit with what they teach in their grade. Too often, new teachers are given very little coaching on curriculum. Some schools pair a new teacher with a mentor, but sometimes this covers only such topics as school operations and procedures. Curricular mapping will give the new teacher more than a textbook or daily schedule of subjects to teach.

> Curricular mapping also helps experienced teachers to have meaningful conversations to ensure a long-range understanding and a deliberate scope and sequence of student learning. Teachers are the experts in lesson preparation and in meeting the needs of the students under their care. The school attempts to multiply the strengths of teachers by designing a comprehensive plan that unites what they are doing individually and departmentally to achieve the school's mission. Having a comprehensive curricular plan and curricular mapping is a strong and positive tool the school can use to explain why its education is so meaningful and important when parents inquire about the school or when present families are considering educational alternatives.

OBJECTIONS FROM ADMINISTRATION

1. Some school heads might be uncomfortable with the new accountability structure for performance and accomplishment.

> Response: Under the mission-directed governance model, the school head is empowered to work with the faculty and staff to accomplish the directions of the board without wondering at each new board meeting whether the priorities have changed or whether there is a new political distraction to cause stress. As a

record of accomplishments develops, the school head has a better opportunity to know expectations and find a sense of satisfaction.

2. The head of school may feel pressured to take full responsibility for whether the school leadership has a vision for the school and is advancing the school toward that vision.

   Response: The head of school does not have to dream up a vision in isolation. The mission-directed model gives the opportunity for all, especially the faculty, to participate in the process of initiating and developing ideas that will more effectively accomplish the mission. When the vision is presented to the board and approved, the board then shares responsibility and accountability for the vision. By using measurement tools, administration and faculty can see and celebrate the improvements that are made over time. Through continual interaction with the faculty and the board, the school head will grow into the vision and be stimulated to recall the purpose for entering education in the first place.

MAKE THE CHANGE: IT'S WORTH IT!

As was stated in an earlier chapter, the first priority of the mission statement is to guide and focus the activity of the organization. A secondary purpose is as a tool to explain the purpose of Christian education to the public, to families who may potentially consider sending their children to the school, and to donors. The mission statement can be used as a marketing tool. Imagine the impact for student recruitment when the school is able to clearly explain the advantages of attending the school, supported by many examples of the programs and experiences that uniquely nurture the student!

A promotional problem that so many Christian schools have is figuring out what is distinctive about the school. Too often school advertising strategies are reduced to promoting general aspirations that apply to competing schools as well. For effective promotion, the Christian school needs to articulate what is distinctive about its education and how its education will affect what the student will learn and become. The school's mission statement and descriptions of distinctive training should be able to be stated by every student, employee, board member, and parent.

How will your school live in this changing world? There are many circumstances outside the control of the school leaders, but the very process of handling change does not have to add to the confusion and unpredictability. The mission-directed governance model is intended to protect and preserve what is dearest to the school community as well as advance and promote the school's mission. The board's accountability is not only to the owner, friends, and parents, but ultimately to Christ.

The mission-directed governance model will not solve all the school's problems; however, this governance model is designed to provide an effective process for handling problems. It contributes to the orderly resolution of problems and goals, making the decision-making process less political. The school leaders will still have to deal with budgets and tuition, student retention and recruitment, discipline, and what students should learn. However, they will face fewer surprises and will no longer jockey for personal or group political advantages. The mission-directed model makes the school work better by defining the nonnegotiables, which must not change; the mission toward which all parties want the school to aspire; the process that delineates roles, authority, responsibility, and accountability; the common goals; and the process of decision making.

The mission-directed governance model provides a process for the school to prepare long-range goals and to guide and even initiate change that brings the school's ministry a little closer to the ideal.

The main emphasis of this book is that the school needs to advance its mission, not just protect and preserve a tradition or merely act in response to consumer demand. The mission-directed governance model is intended to help the school focus on what the school should philosophically advance. Its purpose is to free the school to purposefully and proactively pursue its mission in every area of the school. Is the school in a strong position to take the mission seriously, intentionally identifying what students should learn and pursuing ideas as to what the school must do to provide that training? The goal is to make the mission a force that deliberately infiltrates and saturates the deepest areas of student learning. The mission statement can be so much more than an inspirational theme.

The mission-directed model allows the school to develop a comprehensive schoolwide educational plan. The school needs to develop a comprehensive curriculum that integrates the core curricular principles throughout all subjects. School leadership is challenged to consciously develop experiences, extracurricular offerings, and service opportunities to ensure that students are learning what is indicated in the mission statement. The school leadership needs to analyze its policies and procedures of operation to ensure that they are an extension of the mission.

As a school board considers whether the school should make the change to the mission-directed governance model, the board should anticipate the challenging process that will be required in order to transition to a new governance model. It should anticipate the political pressures and consider the difficulty, hard work, and the many discussions that will be needed in order to implement such a plan. However, note that if the board delays the decision and maintains the school's present traditional governance model or governance-by-policy, it is making a decision.

Any governance decision will have risks and consequences. The board needs to prayerfully review the reasons for considering the change in the first place. Consider the many alternative educational choices available to families, the economic situation, the number of students enrolling, and the amounts of special contributions. Perhaps it is helpful for the board to ask, If this school were just beginning, what governance model would we adopt to meet these challenges and changes? What is the board's best position for enacting responsible stewardship and leadership?

As Christians observe the changes in our society and culture, there is often an anxiety about where these trends will lead. Christian ideals and practices seem to be more sharply challenged. But there are also marvelous opportunities to be witnesses in presenting the gospel in word and action, for individuals as well as for the community. What role is your school preparing your students to take? Is your school purposefully preparing students for their responsibilities and prospects to serve the kingdom of Christ within the society and the culture they live in and confront?

Those involved in Christian education have been entrusted with a treasure. Uniquely Christian education provides training based on Jesus as the way, the truth, and the life (John 14:6). The treasure is not to be buried, merely protected, or hidden. The treasure must be the foundation upon which Christians make new claims and advances. The board has the opportunity to lead and govern an educational community that purposefully nurtures the next generation of Christians to change the world by growing in discipleship and being equipped with vision, understanding, discernment, and service in order to renew all relationships and culture to be under the authority of Jesus Christ. Do Christian education on purpose!

May the Lord bless you as you seek to do His will in your school.

FOR REFLECTION AND DISCUSSION

1. What are some of the issues that have led you to consider governance questions related to your school situation?

2. Who among your school constituency might have reservations about implementing the mission-directed governance model, and for what reasons?

3. Review the steps that you would need to take in order to transition to a mission-directed model of governance.

4. Are there any issues of governance on which your school board, administration, or others agree? Identify and discuss those issues.

5. What should be the first steps in reaching agreement on governance issues?

APPENDIX A

Sample Board Policy Handbook

It is helpful to divide the board policy handbook into tabs by subject area. Boards can determine their own organization of the board policy handbook, but this outline of sample topics may offer a useful beginning point.

Tab 100. Founding and formal documents
- Documents of incorporation and nonprofit status
- Covenant with owner (if owner is an association, identifying who is a member)

Tab 200. School identity, mission, and measurement
- School name
- Mission statement
- Statement of philosophy
- Statement of belief
- School location(s)
- School motto
- School mascot
- School colors
- Educational goals (what the school is trying to cultivate in its students)
- Core curricular principles (the school's educational perspective, which is purposefully integrated throughout the curriculum so that it will lead to accomplishing the educational goals)
- Board statements of what is to be measured and by what means

Tab 300. Governance
- Owner policies
- Board of trustees: the role and limitations of the board, and minimum requirements to serve
- Board of trustees code of conduct (ethics and demeanor expected)
- Cause and process for removing a board member
- Officers of the board, with tasks and limitations
- Board standing committees (if applicable) with their mandates and limitations
- Board education and training

Tab 400. Board and staff policies
- School head's role as sole connection and liaison between board and school operations
- Board's direction of school head by policies
- School head general limitations
- School head communication and reporting to board
- School head evaluation
- School head employment contract

Tab 500. Personnel
- Qualifications and conditions of employment
- Policy of nondiscrimination
- Employee prohibitions
- Conflict of interest
- Employment contracts
- Employment classifications

Tab 600. Education
- Expectation for curriculum with scope and sequence
- Standards of excellence
- Integration of core curricular principles
- Class sizes
- Cocurricular programs
- Special programs (e.g., for students with disabilities and international students)
- Online, home education, and other educational options
- Graduation requirements

Tab 700. Students
- Student expectations
- Student discipleship purpose, limitations, expulsion
- Student off-campus expectations

Tab 800. Admissions
- Minimum criteria for families
- Minimum criteria for students
- Policy of nondiscrimination

Tab 900. Facilities and equipment
- Expectations regarding health and safety and compliance with federal, state, and local regulations

- Requirement for crisis management plan
- Transportation and drivers
- Nonschool use of facilities

Tab 1000. Business and finances
- Insurance
- Confidentiality and security of records and data School head to prepare annual budget (development process and projections of revenue and expenditures)
- Ongoing financial expectations
- Financial reporting
- Employment salary and benefits schedule
- Tuition schedule and financial aid
- Investment limitations

Tab 1100. Home, church, community, and government
- Communication to employees and constituency
- Noncustodial parents
- Church relations
- Community and government relations

Tab 1200. Auxiliary organizations, promotion, development, and strategic planning
- Auxiliary organizations
- School foundation
- Promotion and public relations and limitations
- Development and fund-raising
- Strategic planning

APPENDIX B

Sample Core Curricular Principles

The core curricular principles are written as board policies in order to ensure that the school accomplishes its educational mission. The school will have its overall mission statement. The intention here is to illustrate how it is possible for the board to develop policies that govern the school in accordance with its mission.

> The mission of _____ Christian School is to provide and promote a biblically based, quality education that nurtures the students to grow in God-centered discipleship, equipped with vision, understanding, discernment, and service in order to renew all relationships and culture to be under the authority of Jesus Christ.

The core curricular principles provide the Christian perspective that guides the purpose of each subject area such as mathematics, science, history, and art. Philippians 1:9–11 gives a summary that underscores the purpose of Christ-centered understanding, discernment, and loving service resulting in righteousness that transforms the world for the glory of God:

> And this is my prayer: *that your love may abound* more and more in *knowledge and depth of insight,* so that you may be able *to discern* what is best and may be pure and blameless until the day of Christ, filled with the *fruit of righteousness* that comes through Jesus Christ—to the glory and praise of God. (emphasis added)

Tab 601. The student is to mature and grow in faith, conviction, and commitment to Jesus Christ as Savior and Lord. The student will appropriately respond with worship, piety, character, and integrity. The student will seek to love God and neighbor.

> "Love the Lord your God with all your heart and with all your soul and with all your mind.: This is the first and greatest commandment. And the second is like it: "Love your neighbor as yourself." All the Law and the Prophets hang on these two commandments. (Matthew 22:37–40)

> It was he who gave some to be apostles, some to be prophets, some to be evangelists, and some to be pastors and teachers to prepare God's people for works of service, so that the body of Christ may be built up until we

all reach unity in the faith and in the knowledge of the Son of God and become mature, attaining to the whole measure of the fullness of Christ. (Ephesians 4:11–13)

Whoever wants to be my disciple must deny themselves and take up their cross daily and follow me. (Luke 9:23)

Tab 602. The student will develop understanding.

602.1. The student is to distinguish a Christian faith position from non-Christian religions and philosophies, from views that determine truth only by currently accepted scientific reason, and from views that assume truth is relative to the individual. (With these first core curricular principles, the student is to know the difference between Christianity and other religions, scientism, and relativism. The student will know the difference between historic Christianity of the creeds and the teachings of a cult. The student will know that Jesus Christ is the only way of salvation; syncretism is not an option.)

602.1.1. There is truth (not relativism).
- Exodus 20, Deuteronomy 5 (Ten Commandments)
- Mark 12:28–34; Matthew 22:37–40 (summary of the Law)
- Matthew 7:22, Luke 6:27 (Golden Rule)
- John 14:6–7 (Jesus is the way and the truth and the life.)
- Acts 4:12 (No other name under heaven; no one comes to the Father except through Christ.)

602.1.2. Serve God only.
- Hosea 8:7 (Israel to reap the whirlwind for idolatry)
- I John 5:21 (keep from idols)

602.1.3. All knowledge begins with faith position of the heart.
- Ephesians 4:21–24
- Proverbs 9:10

602.2. The student is to distinguish the characteristics of a biblical worldview. (With these core curricular principles, the student will distinguish the beliefs and characteristics of biblical Christianity and its understanding as whole-life discipleship.)

602.2.1. God is central to the purpose and meaning of life.

602.2.1.1. God is sovereign, and Jesus Christ is Lord over all aspects of life. (This is distinguished from a dualistic sacred/secular position.)

602.2.1.1. God is sovereign.
- Genesis 1:1–2 (God created heaven and earth.)
- Genesis 1:26–28 (God created man and woman in His own image.)

- Isaiah 46:9–10 (God makes known the end from the beginning; His purpose will stand.)
- Psalm 103:19 (The Lord established His throne; His kingdom rules over all.)
- Proverbs 19:21 (There are many plans in a person's heart, but it is the Lord's purpose that prevails.)
- Matthew 10:29 (God watches over sparrows.)
- Ephesians 1:4 (He chose us to be holy and blameless; predestined to be adopted.)
- Ephesians 1:9–10 (He made known the mystery of His will; all things under one head, even Christ)
- Ephesians 1:11 (We are predestined by Him who works out everything in conformity to His will.)
- Ephesians 3:14–21 (May we grasp how immeasurable God's love is; to Him be glory in the church for ever)
- Revelation 18:21 (The great city of Babylon will be thrown down.)
- Revelation 20:7–10 (Satan thrown into the lake of burning sulfur.)
- Revelation 21:1–8 (There will be a new heaven and new earth.)
- Romans 8:29 (Those He predestined He justified, glorified.)
- Romans 9:6–18 (Jacob have I loved, and Esau hated.)
- Ephesians 2:4–5 (God made us alive even when we were dead; saved by grace.)
- Ephesians 1:13–14 (We are sealed by the promise of the Holy Spirit.)
- Romans 8:26–39 (We know in all things God works for good of those who love Him; death can't separate us.)
- 2 Corinthians 1:21–22 (God makes us stand firm; sealed with Spirit in our hearts.)

602.2.1.2. Jesus Christ is Lord of all.

- Colossians 2:9–10 (Christ is fullness of deity who is head over every power and authority.)
- Matthew 28:16–20 (Jesus gives the Great Commission; all authority given to Jesus.)
- Hebrews 1:1–4 (Jesus appointed heir of all; sustaining all things)
- Leviticus 26; Joel 1:15–2:11 (God works through weather.)
- Matthew 19:28–30 (Followers will sit on thrones; those who left family will receive reward.)

602.2.1.3. All of creation exists for the purpose of bringing glory and honor to God. We seek our place of service within His will and plan. (This is distinguished from a view in which God assists us to accomplish our own plans, happiness, or fulfillment.)

- Ephesians 1:7–10 (God bring all things in heaven and on earth under one head—Christ.)
- Ephesians 3:14–21 (To him be glory in the church.)

602.2.2. God reveals Himself to us.

602.2.2.1. Jesus is the Word incarnate. He is Creator, King, Provider, Redeemer, and in Him all things hold together. (This is distinguished from a view in which the role of Jesus is limited to being Savior of the souls of mankind.)

- Colossians 1:15–20 (Christ is supreme.)
- Ephesians 1:15–23 (Christ is seated at God's right hand, above all rule; all things placed under His feet.)
- John 1:1–18 (In the beginning was the Word.)

602.2.2.2. The Bible is God's inspired, infallible, and inerrant Word by which we understand God, His creation, the Fall, salvation, and God's will for our lives. It is to be interpreted as a unified whole. (This is distinguished from views that sharply divide the Testaments, or that see the Bible simply as a set of propositions, a textbook, or one of many religious writings.)

- 2 Peter 1:16–23 (The apostles were eyewitnesses; Scriptures from God.)
- 2 Timothy 3:16 (All Scripture is God-breathed.)
- Matthew 22:37–40 (The greatest commandment; all law and prophets hang on these two commandments.)

602.2.2.3. God reveals Himself through His creation. All of God's revelations are true and are in ultimate harmony. (This is distinguished from a view that allows any of the revelations of God to be considered irrelevant or in disharmony.)

- Romans 1:18–20 (Creation reveals eternal power and divine nature.)
- Psalm 19 (Heavens declare God's glory; law of the Lord is perfect.)

602.3. God's revelations explain the relationships between God, man, and the world.

602.3.1. Creation

602.3.1.1. Creation is good and belongs to God. (This is distinguished from a view in which physical matter is evil, views in which the creation belongs to Satan, and views such as naturalistic evolution in which the world is neutral.)

- John1:3–5 (Christ made the created order.)
- 1 Timothy 1:4–5 (Everything God made is good.)

602.3.1.2. Mankind is created in the image of God and is responsible for bringing all relationships under authority of God, including society and culture. (This is distinguished from a view that suggests that we have a responsibility only with regard to our soul or spirit.)

- Genesis 1:27 (Man was created in image of God.)
- Genesis 1:28–29 (God gives a cultural mandate.)
- Psalm 8:4–8 (Man rules over creation.)

602.3.2. Fall

602.3.2.1. Sin is a condition that affects every relationship. (This is distinguished from a view in which sin affects only personal salvation.)

602.3.2.1.1. All fall short of perfection.

- Psalm 14:3 (All have sinned and turned aside.)
- Psalm 53:3 (Everyone is corrupt.)
- Romans 1:18–32 (People rejected God's revelation.)
- Romans 2:1-3 (We judge others as proof of guilt.)
- Romans 2:12–16 (Our consciences prove our guilt.)
- Romans 3:23 (Wages of sin is death.)
- I John 1:8 (We have sinned.)
- James 2:8–11 (If you break even one law you are lawbreaker.)

602.3.2.1.2. Man's nature is sinful.

- Genesis 3:1–5 (Satan's temptation: you will be like God knowing good and evil.)
- Ephesians 2:1–3 (We were dead in sin, gratifying cravings of our sinful nature.)
- Romans 5:12 (One person's trespass brought condemnation for all, so also one person's righteousness brings life.)
- John 3:6 (Flesh gives birth to flesh, but the Spirit gives birth to spirit.)
- James 1:12–15 (God does not tempt; rather we are tempted by our own evil desire.)

602.2.2.1.3. Mankind is completely sinful.

- Genesis 6:5 (Every inclination of the thoughts of his heart was only evil all the time.)

- Isaiah 64:6 (All of our righteous acts are like filthy rags.)
- John 8:34 (Everyone who sins is a slave to sin.)
- Romans 7:18 (I know that nothing good lives in me, that is, in my sinful nature.)
- Titus 1:15 (To those corrupted, nothing is pure; both minds and consciences are corrupted.)

602.2.2.1.4. Consequences of sin

- Romans 6:23 (The wages of sin is death.)
- James 1:15 (Sin, when it is full-grown, gives birth to death.)
- Ephesians 2:12 (You were separate from Christ, without hope or God.)
- Ephesians 4:18–19 (They were darkened in understanding; have given themselves to impurity.)
- Romans 1:21–28 (Though they knew God, they didn't glorify or thank Him; their thinking became futile.)

602.2.2.1.5. The struggle between right and wrong affects all relationships and calls for both personal and corporate discernment and decision making that includes the call for justice and righteousness. (This is distinguished from a view that suggests sin does not affect our thinking, will, decisions, emotions, and relationships, but leaves people basically and morally good, needing only assistance from God in personal salvation.)

- Genesis 3:17–19 (Cursed is the ground; labor, pain, death.)
- Romans 8:18–27 (Creation groans.)
- Romans 3:9–26 (All have sinned.)

602.3.3. Redemption

602.3.3.1. By God's grace, the death and resurrection of Jesus Christ on the cross paid for the sins of those who believe in Christ.

- John 3:16–17 (Believe on Jesus.)
- Romans 1:17 (The gospel; righteousness by faith.)
- 1 Timothy 1:15–17 (Jesus came to save sinners, of whom I am worst.)
- Romans 10:9–10 (Believe in heart and confess with mouth and be saved.)
- I Corinthians 15 (The resurrection of Jesus ensures our resurrection.)
- Romans 4:22–25 (Jesus was delivered to death for our sins, raised to life for our justification.)

- Hebrews 2:17 (Jesus fully human to make atonement.)
- Acts 4:1 (Salvation is found in no one else.)

602.3.3.2. The Holy Spirit empowers the forgiven believer to live a purposeful life of service in gratitude.

- Romans 7 (Believers are dead to law; struggle with sin.)
- Romans 8:1–17 (There is now no condemnation for those who are in Christ Jesus.)
- James 2:14–26 (Works come as a result of faith.)
- 1 Peter 1:13–16 (Prepare minds for action; be holy.)
- Ephesians 2:8–10 (We are saved by grace; we are God's workmanship to do good works.)
- 2 Corinthians 7:1 (We are to purify ourselves body and spirit out of reverence for God.)
- Matthew 12:15–21 (Jesus fulfills Isaiah, He leads justice to victory.)
- Isaiah 58 (True worship is righteousness and justice.)
- II Corinthians 5:15–21 (We are God's ambassadors to reconcile all things to Him.)
- Psalm 82 (Defend cause of weak and fatherless; you are God's representatives.)
- Micah 6:8 (Act justly and love mercy and walk humbly with your God.)
- Ephesians 4:22–24 (Put off old self and put on new self.)

602.3.3.3. The Christian school calls students to personal faithfulness to Jesus Christ.

- Ephesians 4:17–24 (New thinking; put off old self and put on new self.)
- Romans 12:1–2 (Be living sacrifice.)
- 2 Corinthians 10:5 (Take captive every thought.)
- Matthew 22:37–39 (Jesus gives the greatest commandment.)
- I Thessalonians 5:21–22 (Test everything. Hold on to good, avoid evil.)
- I Peter 1:13–16 (Prepare minds for action; do not conform to evil; be holy.)
- Galatians 5:16–26 (Live by the Spirit; acts of sinful nature; fruit of the Spirit.)

602.3.3.4. Each person is to give thanks to God by loving God above all and one's neighbor as oneself.

- Luke 10:25–28 (Love the Lord with all your heart and love your neighbor as yourself.)
- Ephesians 5:1–2 (Be imitators of God.)
- Colossians 1:9–14 (Live life worthy; joyfully give thanks.)

602.3.3.5. Through God's providence, He continues to love and care for all of creation. (This is distinguished from a dualistic view in which the physical world is evil and the soul is good.)

- 1 Corinthians 3:16-17 (You are God's temple.)
- 1 Corinthians 6:18-20 (Flee sexual immorality; your body is the temple of Holy Spirit.)
- 1 Corinthains15 (The resurrection of the body is a fact.)

602.3.3.6. The redemption of Christ affects all relationships, including creation. (This is distinguished from a view in which the effects of redemption are only personal).

- Revelation 21:1-4 (God prepares new heaven and new earth.)
- 2 Peter 3:10–15 (There will be new heaven and new earth.)

602.3.3.7. Christ will come again.

- Matthew 25:31–46 (Judge divides sheep from goats.)
- Revelation 21 (There will be new heaven and earth.)
- Revelation 19 (Enemies of Jesus thrown into lake of fire.)

602.3.3.8. Each Christian is part of the body of Christ, the Church, and is called to faithfully grow in Christian maturity by actively attending and participating in a local Christian church community. (This is in contrast to those who consider one's relationship with Christ to be only individualistic, not communal.)

- Matthew 28:18–20 (Jesus gives the Great Commission.)
- Ephesians 1:17–23 (Christ is all authority for the church.)
- Ephesians 2: 19–22 (We are built together as a holy temple with Christ as cornerstone.)
- Ephesians 4:1–6 (There is one body and one spirit.)
- Ephesians 4:11–16 (Church leaders to build up believers to be unified in faith and mature.)
- Galatians 3:26–29 (All believers are sons of God—Jew and Greek, male and female, slave and free.)

Tab 603. The student is to grow in discernment, critical thinking, and wise decision making.

603.1. Student is to discern cultures and worldviews, their faith assumptions, and the consequent implications.
- Proverbs 16:21 (The wise in heart are called discerning; pleasant words promote instruction.)
- 1 John 4:1–3 (Do not believe every spirit, but test the spirits to see whether they are from God.)
- 1 Thessalonians 5:21–22 (Test everything. Hold on to the good. Avoid every kind of evil.)
- Romans 12:2 (Be able to test and approve what God's will is.)
- 1 Corinthians 2:16 (The Spirit searches all things…. But we have the mind of Christ.)

603.2. Developing a Christian understanding and worldview will certainly be foundational to our Christian school education. It will help students explore differences between a Christian perspective and perspectives presented by competing religions and philosophies.
- Ephesians 4:14 (Then we will no longer be infants, tossed back and forth by the waves, and blown here and there by every wind of teaching and by the cunning and craftiness of people in their deceitful scheming.)
- Colossians 2:2–3 (In Christ in are hidden all the treasures of wisdom and knowledge.)
- Colossians 2:8 (See to it that no one takes you captive through hollow and deceptive philosophy, which depends on human tradition and the principles of this world rather than on Christ.)
- 2 Corinthians 10:5 (We demolish arguments and every pretension that sets itself up against the knowledge of God, and we take captive every thought to make it obedient to Christ.)

603.3. The student will learn to grow in a biblical culture and worldview.

    603.3.1. Students will seek to develop their mind and life to conform to the biblical view.

    603.3.2. Students will understand the role of the Church universal and institutional church in sin and faithfulness as it interacted with cultures and worldviews.
- Ephesians 1 (Christ gave power to the church.)
- 1 Peter 1:13 (Prepare your minds for action; be self-controlled; set your hope fully on the grace to be given you when Jesus Christ is revealed.)
- Romans 12:2 (Be transformed by the renewing of your mind.)

- Ephesians 4:20–24 (You were taught, with regard to your former way of life, to put off your old self, which is being corrupted by its deceitful desires; to be made new in the attitude of your minds; and to put on the new self, created to be like God in true righteousness and holiness.)
- Matthew 22:37–39 (Jesus replied, "Love the Lord your God with all your heart and with all your soul and with all your mind. This is the first and greatest commandment. And the second is like it: Love your neighbor as yourself.")

603.4. All people know about God through creation, but wicked hearts produce other perspectives and behaviors.

- Ephesians 4:17–19 (So I tell you this, and insist on it in the Lord, that you must no longer live as the Gentiles do, in the futility of their thinking. They are darkened in their understanding and separated from the life of God because of the ignorance that is in them due to the hardening of their hearts. Having lost all sensitivity, they have given themselves over to sensuality so as to indulge in every kind of impurity, with a continual lust for more.)
- Romans 1:21, 25, 28 (For although they knew God; they neither glorified him as God nor gave thanks to him, but their thinking became futile and their foolish hearts were darkened.... They exchanged the truth of God for a lie.... Furthermore, since they did not think it worthwhile to retain the knowledge of God, he gave them over to a depraved mind, to do what ought not to be done.)
- 1 Peter 1:13–16 (Therefore prepare your minds for action; be self-controlled; set your hope fully on the grace to be given you when Jesus Christ is revealed. As obedient children, do not conform to the evil desires you had when you lived in ignorance. But just as he who called you is holy, so be holy in all you do; for it is written: "Be holy, because I am holy.")

Tab 604. The student will be equipped for works of service.

604.1. The student will understand and be prepared for servant leadership.

604.2. Preach the gospel of salvation.

- Mark 16:15–16 ("Go into all the world and preach the good news to all creation. Whoever believes and is baptized will be saved, but whoever does not believe will be condemned.")
- Romans 10:15 (How, then, can they call on the one they have not believed in? And how can they believe in the one of whom they have not heard? And how can they hear without someone preaching to them? And can they preach unless they are sent?)

- James 2:14–18 (What good is it, my brothers, if a man claims to have faith but has no deeds?)

604.3. Christians are called to bring justice, righteousness, and reconciliation.

- Ephesians 4:24 (Put on the new self, created to be like God in true righteousness and holiness.)
- Ephesians 2:10) (We are God's workmanship, created in Christ Jesus to do good works, which God prepared in advance for us to do.)
- Philippians 2:13 (It is God who works in you to will and to act according to His good purpose.)
- Ephesians 5:15 (Be very careful, then, how you live—not as unwise but as wise, making the most of every opportunity, because the days are evil.)
- Colossians 4:5 (Be wise in the way you act toward outsiders; make the most of every opportunity.)
- 2 Corinthians 5:17–21 (Therefore, if anyone is in Christ, he is a new creation; the old has gone, the new has come. All this is from God, who reconciled us to himself through Christ and gave us the ministry of reconciliation: that God was reconciling the world to himself in Christ, not counting men's sins against them. And he has committed to us the message of reconciliation. We are therefore Christ's ambassadors, as though God were making his appeal through us. We implore you on Christ's behalf: Be reconciled to God. God made him who had no sin to be sin for us, so that in him we might become the righteousness of God.)
- Matthew 5:13–16 (You are the salt of the earth. You are the light of the world. Let your light shine before others, that they may see your good deeds and praise your Father in heaven.)
- Micah 6:8 (He has showed you, O man, what is good. And what does the Lord require of you? Act justly and love mercy and walk humbly with your God.)
- Luke 10:25–37 (Jesus tells the parable of the good Samaritan.)
- Matthew 10:42 (Give cup of cold water.)
- Isaiah 1:17 (Stop doing wrong, learn to do right! Seek justice, encourage the oppressed. Defend the cause of the fatherless, plead the case of the widow.)
- Isaiah 61:3–4 (They will be called oaks of righteousness, a planting of the Lord for the display of His splendor. They will rebuild the ancient

ruins and restore the places long devastated; they will renew the ruined cities that have been devastated for generations.)

- Matthew 23:23 (Woe to you, teachers of the law and Pharisees, you hypocrites! You give a tenth of our spices—mint, dill and cumin. But you have neglected the more important matters of the law—justice, mercy and faithfulness.)
- Galatians 6:10 (Therefore, as we have opportunity, let us do good to all people, especially to those who belong to the family of believers.)
- Isaiah 58: 6–9 (Is not this the kind of fasting I have chosen: to loose the chains of injustice and untie the cords of the yoke, to set the oppressed free and break every yoke? Is it not to share your food with the hungry and to provide the poor wanderer with shelter—when you see the naked, to clothe him, and not to turn away from your own flesh and blood? Then your light will break forth like the dawn, and your healing will quickly appear; then your righteousness will go before you, and the glory of the Lord will be your rear guard. Then you will call, and the Lord will answer; you will cry for help, and He will say: Here am I.)
- Amos 5:21–24 (I hate, I despise your religious feasts; I cannot stand your assemblies. Even though you bring me burnt offerings and grain offerings, I will not accept them. Though you bring choice fellowship offerings, I will have no regard for them. Away with the noise of your songs! I will not listen to the music of your harps. But let justice roll on like a river, righteousness like a never-failing stream!)

Tab 605. The student will understand that the school is designed to help parents raise their children to accept Jesus Christ as Savior and Lord and to ensure that their children become mature Christians who are prepared for works of service to carry out the Great Commission and advance the reality of Christ's kingdom.
- Deuteronomy 6 (The Lord God is one; impress on children.)
- Exodus 20:12 (Honor father and mother.)
- Deuteronomy 5:16 (Honor father and mother.)
- Proverbs (Train a child.)
- Ephesians 6:1–4 (Children, obey parents.)
- Col 3:20 (Children, obey parents.)
- Matthew 19:13–15 (Little children come to Jesus.)

SUMMARY OF CURRICULAR STRATEGY

The following gives a curricular strategy to develop student learning of the core curricular principles and their biblical support:

Early elementary

- Students learn that the Bible is God's Word and is the rule of faith and obedience.
- Students memorize verses that support the core curricular principles.
- Students become familiar with a description of the core curricular principles (phrased for early elementary students).

Middle elementary

- Students continue to memorize the verses that support the core curricular principles.
- Students become familiar with the core curricular principles as summarizing the Bible passages.
- Students connect and match verses and the specific core curricular principles.

Middle school

- Students write essays about the core curricular principles using appropriate Bible passages.

High school

- Students learn to defend core curricular principles against opposing positions.

WORKS CITED

Carver, John. 1997. *Boards that make a difference: A new design for leadership in nonprofit organizations.* 2nd ed. San Francisco: Jossey-Bass.

Collins, Jim. 2001. *Good to great: Why some companies make the leap…and others don't.* New York: HarperCollins.

Marsden, George M. 1994. *The soul of the American university: From Protestant establishment to established nonbelief.* New York: Oxford University Press.